The Organization for Security and Co-operation in Europe

This book examines the development and evolution of the Organization of Security and Co-operation (OSCE) in Europe (formerly the CSCE) during and after the Cold War.

During the Cold War, the two global superpowers were able to come together to resolve many issues of transparency and common challenges, leading to a change in European and global security. The OSCE covered the area formerly occupied by NATO and the Warsaw Pact, championing the Helsinki Final Act, which became a key international instrument to encourage peace and security. Following the end of the Cold War, the OSCE became a key institution positioned between the European Union and NATO, focusing on furthering democracy, protecting human and minority rights, and encouraging military reform in a drastically dynamic region.

The Organization for Security and Co-operation in Europe sheds light on an institution that changed the face of global security during the Cold War and championed the rise of democratization in Central and Eastern Europe as well as the former Soviet republics following the collapse of the Soviet Union. This book will appeal to students, scholars and others interested in global governance, security studies, European politics, and international relations.

David J. Galbreath is Lecturer in Politics and International Relations at the University of Aberdeen, UK.

Routledge Global Institutions

Edited by Thomas G. Weiss
The CUNY Graduate Center, New York, USA
and Rorden Wilkinson
University of Manchester, UK

About the Series

The Global Institutions Series is designed to provide readers with comprehensive, accessible, and informative guides to the history, structure, and activities of key international organizations. Every volume stands on its own as a thorough and insightful treatment of a particular topic, but the series as a whole contributes to a coherent and complementary portrait of the phenomenon of global institutions at the dawn of the millennium.

Books are written by recognized experts, conform to a similar structure, and cover a range of themes and debates common to the series. These areas of shared concern include the general purpose and rationale for organizations, developments over time, membership, structure, decision-making procedures, and key functions. Moreover, the current debates are placed in an historical perspective alongside informed analysis and critique. Each book also contains an annotated bibliography and guide to electronic information as well as any annexes appropriate to the subject matter at hand.

The volumes currently published or under contract include:

The United Nations and Human Rights (2005)
A guide for a new era
by Julie Mertus (American University)

The UN Secretary–General and Secretariat (2005)
by Leon Gordenker (Princeton University)

United Nations Global Conferences (2005)
by Michael G. Schechter (Michigan State University)

The UN General Assembly (2005)
by M.J. Peterson (University of Massachusetts, Amherst)

Internal Displacement (2006)
Conceptualization and its consequences
by Thomas G. Weiss (The CUNY Graduate Center) and David A. Korn

Global Environmental Institutions (2006)
by Elizabeth R. DeSombre (Wellesley College)

The International Labour
Organization
*by Steve Hughes (University of
Newcastle)*

The Commonwealth(s) and Global
Governance
*by Timothy Shaw (Royal Roads
University)*

UNHCR
The politics and practice of refugee
protection into the twenty-first
century
*by Gil Loescher (University of Oxford),
James Milner (University of Oxford),
and Alexander Betts (University of
Oxford)*

The International Organization for
Standardization and the Global
Economy
Setting standards
*by Craig Murphy (Wellesley College)
and JoAnne Yates (Massachusetts
Institute of Technology)*

The International Olympic Committee
*by Jean-Loup Chappelet (IDHEAP
Swiss Graduate School of Public
Administration) and
Brenda Kübler-Mabbott*

The European Union
*by Clive Archer (Manchester
Metropolitan University)*

The World Health Organization
*by Kelley Lee (London School of
Hygiene and Tropical Medicine)*

Internet Governance
The new frontier of global institutions
*by John Mathiason (Syracuse
University)*

Shaping the Humanitarian World
by Peter Walker (Tufts University)

Contemporary Human Rights Ideas
*by Bertrand G. Ramcharan (Geneva
Graduate Institute of International
Studies)*

For further information regarding the series, please contact:

Craig Fowlie, Publisher, Politics & International Studies
Taylor & Francis
2 Park Square, Milton Park, Abingdon
Oxfordshire OX14 4RN, UK

+44 (0)207 842 2057 Tel
+44 (0)207 842 2302 Fax

craig.fowlie@tandf.co.uk
www.routledge.com

The Organization for Security and Co-operation in Europe

David J. Galbreath

Routledge
Taylor & Francis Group

LONDON AND NEW YORK

First published 2007
by Routledge
2 Park Square, Milton Park, Abingdon, Oxon OX14 4RN

Simultaneously published in the USA and Canada
by Routledge
270 Madison Avenue, New York, NY 10016

Routledge is an imprint of the Taylor & Francis Group, an informa business

© 2007 David J. Galbreath

Typeset in Times New Roman by
Taylor & Francis Books
Printed and bound in Great Britain by
MPG Books Ltd, Bodmin

British Library Cataloguing in Publication Data
A catalogue record for this book is available from the British Library

Library of Congress Cataloging in Publication Data
A catalog record has been requested for this book

ISBN 978–0–415–40763–2 (hbk)
ISBN 978–0–415–40764–9 (pbk)
ISBN 978–0–203–96094–3 (ebk)

For Nicolaas

Contents

Illustrations

Figure

Maps

Boxes

Foreword

The current volume is the fourteenth in a new and dynamic series on "global institutions." The series strives (and, based on the initial volumes, we believe, succeeds) to provide readers with definitive guides to the most visible aspects of what we know as "global governance." Remarkable as it may seem, there exist relatively few books that offer in-depth treatments of prominent global bodies and processes, much less an entire series of concise and complementary volumes. Those that do exist are either out of date, inaccessible to the non-specialist reader, or seek to develop a specialized understanding of particular aspects of an institution or process rather than offering an overall account of its functioning. Similarly, existing books have often been written in highly technical language or have been crafted "in-house" and are notoriously self-serving and narrow.

The advent of electronic media has helped by making information, documents, and resolutions of international organizations more widely available, but it has also complicated matters. The growing reliance on the Internet and other electronic methods of finding information about key international organizations and processes has served, ironically, to limit the educational materials to which most readers have ready access—namely, books. Public relations documents, raw data, and loosely refereed websites do not make for intelligent analysis. Official publications compete with a vast amount of electronically available information, much of which is suspect because of its ideological or self-promoting slant. Paradoxically, a growing range of purportedly independent websites offering analyses of the activities of particular organizations has emerged, but one inadvertent consequence has been to frustrate access to basic, authoritative, critical, and well-researched texts. The market for such has actually been reduced by the ready availability of varying-quality electronic materials.

For those of us who teach, research, and practice in the area, this access to information has been at best frustrating. We were delighted, then, when Routledge saw the value of a series of books that bucks this trend and provides key reference points to the most significant global institutions. They are betting that serious students and professionals will want serious analyses. We have assembled a first-rate line-up of authors to address that market. Our intention, then, is to provide one-stop shopping for all readers—students (both undergraduate and postgraduate), interested negotiators, diplomats, practitioners from nongovernmental and intergovernmental organizations, and other interested parties alike—seeking information about the most prominent institutional aspects of global governance.

The Organization for Security and Co-operation in Europe

Much of the literature of international relations—historical, political, economic, sociological, or legal—deals directly or implicitly with the capacity of institutions to react to changing circumstances and to adapt themselves or languish. It is by now a truism that the end of the Cold War dramatically changed world politics. In addition to the North Atlantic Treaty Organization (the topic of another book in this series published earlier this year),[1] no other institution faced a more radically different agenda than the Organization (at the time, the "Conference") for Security and Cooperation in Europe (OSCE) before and after the fall of the Berlin Wall.

In conceiving a series about global institutions in the twenty-first century, it was clear that a volume about the nuts-and-bolts of the OSCE would be required, and we were pleased with an imaginative proposal from David Galbreath. In the pages that follow, the reader finds an authoritative yet readable introduction to the OSCE's past, present, and future by an up-and-coming scholar of European institutions and politics.

David has been a lecturer at the University of Aberdeen since 2004, following teaching assignments at the Universities of Sheffield, Leeds, and Memphis. Having studied Soviet politics and post-Soviet state, his first book examined the nation-building and minority politics in two former Soviet states.[2] What better preparation, we asked, for someone to take a fresh look at an institution that had begun by finessing questions of human rights and nationalities in the former Soviet bloc?

The Organization for Security and Co-operation in Europe contains the essential nuts-and-bolts as well as the institutional politics circumscribing the transformation of a "conference" to an "organization" that is essential to everything from field operations on the ground in the Balkans and to policy debates in the capitals of both the old and new

Europe. Moreover, the host of linkages to other organizations with a predominant role in Europe—not just NATO but also the European Union, the Western European Union, and others—are found in this concise and user-friendly volume.

We were pleased when David accepted our offer to contribute this book to the series, and we are delighted with the results. He has produced an insightful volume that charts the OSCE's path through the congested terrain of the Cold War and post-Cold War periods. It is a first-rate book: informative, knowledgeable, and considered. We know that those who have come to expect the highest standards from our books will not be disappointed. We are pleased to recommend it to all. As always, comments and suggestions from our readers are welcome.

Thomas G. Weiss, The CUNY Graduate Center, New York, USA
Rorden Wilkinson, University of Manchester, UK
January 2007

Acknowledgements

After several years of teaching and writing on the Organization for Security and Co-operation in Europe (OSCE), it was very good to be able to write this book. The Conference on Security and Cooperation in Europe (CSCE) and the OSCE say much about regional and global politics, Détente, the evolutions of international organizations, and the challenges of the post-Cold War era. And for these reasons, the OSCE is a fascinating subject for study. Nevertheless, many in Western Europe and North America have forgotten about the OSCE. Many times I have been asked during the course of writing this book what I am working on only to be confronted with blank faces and typical responses such as, "The OECD?" I would reply, "Used to be the Conference on Security and Cooperation in Europe." Still nothing. No doubt I have bored many, but I have also intrigued patient listeners and students at the University of Aberdeen who find the insecurities in the post-Cold War era interesting. I hope this book will intrigue others elsewhere as well as lay a foundation for future research on this dynamic organization in a dynamic region.

This book was made possible and helped along by many and I would like to name a few. First, I would like to thank the editors of the *Global Institutions* series for Routledge, Thomas G. Weiss at CUNY Graduate Center in New York and Rorden Wilkinson at the University of Manchester, for giving me the opportunity to write on the OSCE. I also greatly appreciate their comments and remarks regarding earlier drafts. Second, I would like to thank Clive Archer at Manchester Metropolitan University for his willingness to read an early draft. Likewise, I would like to thank Trevor Salmon and James Wyllie at the University of Aberdeen for their comments. Third, I would like to thank the British Academy for their financial support of the project "EU Enlargement and the Minority Rights Regime? The Prospect for Value Transfer in Central and Eastern Europe" (SG-40844). The support of the British Academy allowed me to do interviews in The Hague and Vienna for this book. I would also like to thank the University of Aberdeen College of Arts and Social Sciences who financially supported my fieldwork on this topic.

In terms of fieldwork, I benefited greatly from those people I met in the OSCE. I greatly appreciate the assistance of the Office of the High Commissioner on National Minorities in The Hague as well as Ambassador Rolf Ekeus for taking the time to meet me. In Vienna, I would like to thank the delegations to the OSCE from the UK, Belgium, Russia, Estonia, and Latvia. In the UK delegation, I would like to especially thank Andrew Ford, Stuart Adam and Group Captain Pete Whitaker for sharing their advice and knowledge of the OSCE as well as allowing me access to the Permanent Council meetings. At the OSCE, I gratefully acknowledge the time given to me for interviews in the OSCE Secretariat, Forum for Security Cooperation, Conflict Prevention Centre, and the offices of the Representative on Freedom of the Media. Finally, I would like to thank Pascal Heyman, Deputy Permanent Representative at the Delegation of Belgium to the OSCE for taking the time to meet me and correcting my use of the term "national minorities." The views expressed in this book do not necessarily represent any of those interviewed and are solely the responsibility of the author.

Above all, I would to thank my wife Jolene, whom I often left for fieldwork while she was pregnant with our son. In this regard, I would like to thank my son Nicolaas for setting such a tough book deadline of his birth. I made it.

Abbreviations

CCIAT	Criminal Codes Implementation Assessment Team
CFE Treaty	Conventional Forces in Europe Treaty
CFSP	Common Foreign and Security Policy
CiO	OSCE Chairman-in-Office
CIS	Commonwealth of Independent States
CPC	Conflict Prevention Centre
CSBM	Confidence- and Security-Building Measures
CSCE	Conference on Security and Cooperation in Europe
CSO	Council of Senior Officials
ECSC	European Coal and Steel Community
ENVSEC	Environment and Security Initiative
ESDP	European Security and Defence Policy
EU	European Union
FCNM	Council of Europe Framework Convention for the Protection of National Minorities
FOM	OSCE Representative on Freedom of the Media
FSC	Forum for Security Cooperation
FYR	former Yugoslav Republic
HCNM	OSCE High Commissioner on National Minorities
HLPG	High Level Planning Group
KFOR	NATO Kosovo Force
KLA	Kosovo Liberation Army
MAD	mutually assured destruction
MBFR	Mutual and Balanced Force Reductions
NATO	North Atlantic Treaty Organization
NGO	non-governmental organization
ODIHR	OSCE Office for Democratic Institutions and Human Rights
OSCE	Organization for Security and Co-operation in Europe

PA	OSCE Parliamentary Assembly
PC	OSCE Permanent Council
PfP	Partnership for Peace (NATO)
REACT	Rapid Expert Assistance and Cooperation Teams
SFOR	NATO Stabilization Force in Bosnia-Herzegovina
START	Strategic Arms Reduction Treaty
UN	United Nations
UNHCR	United Nations High Commissioner for Refugees
UNMIK	United Nations [Interim Administration] Mission in Kosovo
USSR	Union of Soviet Socialist Republics
WEU	Western European Union

Introduction

Arguably, no international organization represents the evolution of the insecurities that have faced Europe, Central Asia and North America better than the Organization for Security and Co-operation in Europe (OSCE). This organization spans "from Vancouver to Vladivostok," covering a broad range of countries, cultures and contexts. Initially known as the Conference on Security and Cooperation in Europe (CSCE), the organization began as a way to bring together opposing superpowers to work towards the common goal of security and cooperation in the Euro-Atlantic area. This goal is exhibited in the founding CSCE Helsinki Final Act which has become a key international instrument to encourage peace and security. The formation of the CSCE was the result of significant changes that came about in the Cold War typically referred to as Détente. In the Cold War, the CSCE changed the face of global security by altering the contest from a zero-sum game (I win, you lose) to a positive-sum game (either we all win, or at least no-one loses). Within the CSCE, the two global superpowers were able to come together to resolve many issues of transparency and common challenges. This cooperation led to a change in European and thus global security.

Following the end of the Cold War, the "conference" evolved into the "organization" to become a key organization in furthering democracy, protecting human and minority rights, and encouraging military reform in a drastically dynamic region. In order to take on these challenges, the forerunning CSCE had to develop new institutions and redefine their issue orientation. The end of the Cold War also brought about a dynamic change in the organization itself beginning in 1990. Evolving from a series of summits into an institutionalized political organization came about with the creation of a CSCE Secretariat, the Council of Ministers, the Council of Senior Officials, and the Office for Free Elections. In 1992, the CSCE created other institutions and refined existing ones. For example, the Council of Senior Officials was renamed the Permanent Council while the CSCE High Commission on National Minorities was created anew. At this time, the normative framework of a new security organization had already been created. In 1994, the CSCE was renamed the Organization for Security and Co-operation in Europe to represent its evolved state.

The OSCE's work centered on two inclusive issue areas. First, the OSCE continued to focus on traditional insecurities in the region such as promoting confidence- and security-building measures (CSBMs) in the Euro-Atlantic area. At the same time, the OSCE has developed to engage with a wider scope of insecurities such as internal conflict, i.e. civil wars and ethnic conflict, terrorism, organized crime, and human trafficking. While the original Helsinki Final Act mandated a perpetual conference on security and cooperation in Europe, the OSCE has gone much further in managing insecurities in the Euro-Atlantic area. The OSCE has regularly worked alongside other organizations in its pursuit of security in the area such as the North Atlantic Treaty Organization (NATO) and the United Nations (UN). Second, the OSCE has been able to redefine its engagement of the human dimension by explicitly supporting democracy and human rights in the Euro-Atlantic area's transitioning states. Originally focusing on free elections, the OSCE has developed institutions to deal with a great range of issues such as democratic governance, internal center–periphery relations, increased civic participation in politics, and respect for human and minority rights. Likewise, the OSCE has worked with a great number of other international organizations and non-governmental organizations (NGOs) such as the European Union (EU), the Council of Europe and the International Red Cross.

In managing security and promoting democracy and human rights, the OSCE has developed a mechanism for deploying field missions in participating states where required. Since 1992, the OSCE has had 27 field missions and other field activities focusing on issues from border monitoring to supporting parent–teacher programs in local schools. There are field missions today in such countries as Bosnia-Herzegovina, Georgia, Moldova, and the Former Yugoslav Republic (FYR) of Macedonia. The OSCE has field centers in places like Kazakhstan, Tajikistan, Albania, and Ukraine. Finally, the OSCE has offices in Armenia, Azerbaijan, and Belarus. As illustrated by the OSCE field activities, the majority of the organization's work has been aimed at the area referred to as "East of Vienna." Despite secessionist movements, terrorist attacks, and sour state–minority relations in the West, the OSCE has overwhelmingly remained oriented towards the

East. Only recently has the OSCE begun to observe elections in participating states in the West. Overall, the OSCE remains an inclusive organization in the Euro-Atlantic area with a wide-ranging approach to security and democratic governance as well as an expansive geographic presence.

This book is the first to offer a comprehensive view of the OSCE from its origin and trace its development, as well as question its role in the future European security architecture. While there have been numerous studies on the CSCE/OSCE, they have largely been limited in scope. The lack of a more inclusive narrative is surprising since the OSCE has been a cornerstone organization in relation to the Cold War, the collapse of both the Union of Soviet Socialist Republics (USSR) and Yugoslavia, and past and future EU enlargements. In the beginning, the CSCE represented the change in the way states thought about threats and insecurities in the Cold War. The CSCE focused on the notion of "common and comprehensive security." This is not to say that rivalries did not continue, as the US response to the Soviet invasion of Afghanistan demonstrates, but rather, the organization that has come to be known as the OSCE worked first of all as an organization for political communication during a dynamic era of international politics. Finally, a comprehensive view is important because the OSCE has been an innovative organization without the customary bureaucratic "baggage" of other organizations.

Why study the OSCE? The *Global Institutions* series is based on the premise that international organizations both matter and are actors in their own right in the international system. The OSCE fits within the traditional sense of an intergovernmental organization as opposed to an NGO. Following the Second World War, international organizations have become an increasing part of the international *politique*. The process of globalization has increased the level of activity for these organizations in the international system. States rely on international organizations to produce collective goods that most, if not all, states would not be able to provide alone. Most simply, international organizations allow states to work in concert. Yet, often because of the need for efficiency, increased workload, and fundamentally the political will, international organizations become more than just subjects of international politics but also actors themselves, while not completely losing their inter-governmental dimension. Whether as subjects or actors of international politics, these international organizations are worth studying.

The OSCE fits well into this description. As we shall see, the organization offers its participating states a great deal of collective goods. As the CSCE did before it, the OSCE promotes confidence and security in the region through dialogue and agreed standards, such as monitoring troop movements or military exercises. Second, the OSCE provides epistemic, or knowledge-based, input for participating states in issue areas such as policing, tackling organized crime, election monitoring and promoting inter-ethnic harmony. Third, the OSCE has developed a method of "quiet diplomacy" seen most clearly at work in the OSCE High Commissioner on National Minorities. "Quiet diplomacy" allows the OSCE to act as a third-party broker between opposing political actors. Fourth, and in connection, the OSCE provides a concentrated focus on the status of national minorities, unlike any other international organization. Every conflict in the post-Cold War Europe has been the result of tensions between ethnic groups. Again, the OSCE works as a third-party broker in these situations rather than necessarily as an advocate. Finally, the OSCE provides a field presence unlike any other organization in the Euro-Atlantic area. While many other international organizations engage with the same issue areas, they do so in different ways and are limited in their geographic reach. The OSCE remains the only regional political organization that includes all the states from "Vancouver to Vladivostok."

Layout of the book

The origins of the Helsinki Final Act and the CSCE are firmly rooted in the era of Détente. This book engages with the question of what led to the creation of the CSCE. The book also engages with the way the CSCE transformed itself into the OSCE to face the new challenges of the post-Cold War order. We look at the key institutions that have developed and the actors who have shaped them. We also look at the politics behind the organization, such as Russia's early belief that the OSCE could transcend and ultimately replace NATO as the key security alliance in the region. Finally, the book offers an answer to the question regarding the OSCE's future: does it have a place in the contemporary European security architecture? The following pages will support the argument that not only has the OSCE been an innovative and important organization, but it continues to play an important role in "security and cooperation" in Europe today.

To understand the CSCE, we must understand the organization's founding document and the series of meetings that produced it. The Helsinki Final Act is perhaps one of the most important achievements of the CSCE. While the CSCE does have its roots in the Cold War, the Final Act has stood the test of time and remains an important international document that has had a wide-ranging organizational and legal effect. The Final Act marks a transition from collective security to common security in the Cold War period. Within the Final Act, we can see the "give and take" between the East and West. As we shall see in Chapter 2, this compromise is illustrated in the Final Act's three baskets. Basket I was aimed at confidence-building measures in terms of strategic security on both sides. We have seen these measures taken forward by the post-Cold War OSCE as well as NATO's Partnership for Peace program (PfP). Basket II was aimed at enhancing collaboration in economics, science, and technology and the environment. Such collaboration can also be seen in the efforts of the Council of Europe. Finally, Basket III addressed areas of democracy and human rights. As we shall see, while the Helsinki Final Act was supposed to maintain the status quo and thus alleviate the threat of Western threats to the Soviet Bloc, Basket III was taken by many opponents of the socialist regimes to eventually change the regimes from inside. In John Lewis Gaddis's reflection on the Cold War, he argues, "Helsinki became, in short, a legal and moral trap ... Begun by the Kremlin in an effort to legitimize Soviet control in that part of the World, the Helsinki process became the basis for legitimizing *opposition* to Soviet rule."[1] Finally, the "Decalogue" concentrated on threat reduction, confidence building, and non-intervention as well as further emphasizing areas of human rights. As Chapter 2 will illustrate, the Helsinki Final Act has gone from a mere cooperation agreement in a period of easing tensions in the Cold War to an important political instrument that has changed the way we look at international law, security, and human rights.

The CSCE was predicated on the context of the Cold War. The organization promoted political communication between opposing sides, not to mention a significant number of neutral actors. Like the questions raised about NATO following the end of the Cold War, why should we not expect to see the end of the CSCE and its replacement by a new organization that would be better able to deal with the problems of post-Cold War Europe? In effect, this is what happened. Chapter 3 discusses the transformation and institutionalization of the "Conference" into the "Organization." Even before the collapse of the Central European socialist regimes in the late 1980s, we can see the CSCE beginning to focus on new initiatives for peace and security in the region. This development was largely to do with the rise to power of Mikhail Gorbachev in 1985. In order to chart the transition from conference to organization, Chapter 3 pays special attention to the Stockholm Agreement (1986), the Charter of Paris (1990), the Vienna Document (1990), the Helsinki Summit (1992), and finally the Budapest

Summit (1994) where the CSCE became the OSCE. In Chapter 3, we also focus on the broadened powers of the OSCE and the proliferation of mechanisms to treat new insecurities in post-Cold War Europe and Eurasia. Focusing on delegated responsibilities in the OSCE, we pay attention to the development of operational structures and institutions such as the Secretariat as well as the main decision-making bodies such as the Permanent Council. By discussing the core institutions of the OSCE, Chapter 3 introduces the key organizational issue-areas that are to be explored in Chapters 4 and 5. These activities are conflict prevention, arms control, border management, combating terrorism, anti-trafficking, and democratization.

The majority of OSCE operations have taken place in the former Soviet Union and the former Yugoslavia. While potential and actual conflicts in the former Soviet Union have been numerous, the main focus of Europe's attention has been on the conflicts in the former Yugoslavia. The majority of the OSCE work in these areas has been in long-term missions in the field and the capacity for conflict prevention. Chapter 4 engages with the methods and instruments of the OSCE and their implementation in the field. The chapter looks at six case studies: three in the former Soviet Union and three in the former Yugoslavia. In the former Soviet Union, Chapter 4 looks at Nagorno-Karabakh, Georgia, and Moldova, the so-called "frozen conflicts." Russia's role in these areas is key to their continuation as well as their resolution. Whether as an actor or as a peace-keeper, the Russian Federation has been a primary actor in the "frozen conflicts." In our examination, we will see that OSCE activities are often limited by Russia's profound involvement in these areas. Finally, in the former Yugoslavia, we look at Croatia, Kosovo, and Serbia. The conflicts in the former Yugoslavia have been the most violent in the former socialist bloc. Yet, today Croatia is headed towards EU accession and Kosovo towards independence, while Serbia is rebuilding itself after three conflicts and the recent secession of Montenegro. Overall, the six case studies illustrate the OSCE's ability to deal with hard or traditional security issues. At the same time, it illustrates the OSCE's limitations when it comes to exacting a successful peace resolution.

The OSCE has also turned its attention to soft or non-traditional security issues. Chapter 5 will look at how the OSCE has developed mechanisms to deal with the promotion of democratization and human rights. In this examination, we focus on the actions of the Office for Democratic Institutions and Human Rights, the High Commissioner on National Minorities, and the Representative on Freedom of the Media. In general, considerable attention is given to the role of the OSCE in promoting democracy and the protection of human and minority rights in Central and Eastern Europe. As just one of several European organizations encouraging liberal reforms in the region, we look at the OSCE's role in European enlargement and regional integration. We also look at the OSCE's most innovative mechanism, the High Commissioner. Chapter 5 examines the "quiet diplomacy" of the High Commissioner on National Minorities and the office's role in reformulating standards of minority rights protection. Finally, this chapter examines the OSCE's role in the 2004 enlargement of the EU and NATO. Specifically, Chapter 5 discusses OSCE field activities in six countries. In the former Soviet Union, we look at Latvia, Ukraine, and Kyrgyzstan, and in the former Yugoslavia, we look at Bosnia-Herzegovina and Macedonia. We also look at Albania, our one case study outside the former federated states. These case studies put the OSCE's approach to democratization and human rights in context.

Developing from the previous chapters, Chapter 6 looks at the OSCE's role in the European security architecture. Keeping this focus in mind, the chapter looks at the contribution of the CSCE to the period of Détente and the end of the Cold War. Also, we look at the evolving role of the CSCE in promoting security and cooperation in the Euro-Atlantic area amidst state collapse in the Soviet Union and Yugoslavia. Chapter 6 brings together the institutional and case study chapters to illustrate this development. Particular attention is paid to the OSCE's CSBMs, epistemic input, "quiet diplomacy," and the focus on national minorities. Furthermore, Chapter 6 looks at the OSCE relationship with the other regional international organizations as well as the UN. The discussion raises questions of collaboration and competition. In this regard, the chapter illustrates the increased collaboration between the OSCE and other organizations such as the EU, NATO and the Council of Europe, particularly in relation to the peace-building missions in the former Yugoslavia. The chapter illustrates how the OSCE completes a web of organizations aimed at managing security and promoting democratic governance in Europe.

Whether through conflict resolution such as the observation missions or conflict prevention such as the work of the High Commissioner, we will be able to see the role that the OSCE has carved out for itself in the post-Cold War era. With the evidence provided in the previous chapters, Chapter 7 will answer the question with which we started: Does the OSCE still have a role to play in Europe's contemporary security architecture? In order to answer this question, we reflect on the drawbacks of the OSCE and its effectiveness in the field.

We also engage with contemporary criticisms of the OSCE and argue that the organization remains an important player within the European security architecture. Finally, we look at the prospect that the OSCE may be used as a model for regional security mechanisms for other regions.

From the beginning, the OSCE has been an innovative organization, particularly during a time of constant insecurity as in the Cold War. While the "Conference" was part of the Détente era, it has transcended this international context while at the same time maintaining many of its key objectives as a central part of the organization's *raison d'être*. The founding Helsinki Final Act has lasted as an important international agreement that marked a change in the Cold War and international law. As European security changed, so did the CSCE. With the collapse of the socialist regimes in Central and Eastern Europe as well as the Soviet Union, the CSCE's focus on common security reached new proportions. No longer was the OSCE worried about international conflict directed by the superpowers, but instead was concerned with the insecurities of regime transition and state collapse. In many cases, these insecurities took on the form of contested territorial ownership such as in the disputed region of Nagorno-Karabakh or nationalist aspirations such as in Abkhazia or Croatia. Furthermore, the OSCE took on the role of democracy building and the protection of human rights.[2] Importantly, democracy and democratization had become securitized in that regional organizations began to assume that a democratic Europe would be a peaceful and stable Europe. Based on this assumption, the OSCE has attempted to promote the development of democratic norms and values throughout the Euro-Atlantic area.

Nevertheless, as regional organizations continue to converge in their aims, objectives, and fundamentally their responsibilities, the OSCE finds itself one of many organizations that help ensure peace and stability in the region. There are significant overlapping memberships throughout the EU, NATO, the Council of Europe and the OSCE. With the latest rounds of EU and NATO enlargement, we see the OSCE continue to look further east in its aim of countering insecurities. It is in the countries that are not in or are headed towards membership of these organizations where the OSCE continues to be much needed. As we shall see in the chapters ahead, the OSCE remains an important contributor to the overall European security architecture.

1 European security and cooperation in context

In 1973, states from across Europe, North America, and Eurasia came together to work out an agreement that would promote security and cooperation in Europe. The talks that lasted until 1975 are referred to as the Helsinki Process and they culminated in the Helsinki Final Act, creating the CSCE. However, much had happened up to this point that allowed for the opportunity of security and cooperation in Europe. Following two world wars, neither security nor cooperation looked especially promising when the Cold War began following the end of the Second World War in 1945. In fact, the United States and the Soviet Union would put as much effort into competing in a "cold" war as they had put into fighting a "hot" war. This Cold War between the two post-war superpowers would dominate the remaining part of the twentieth century and would bring the world close to nuclear oblivion at least once. Nevertheless, the Cold War was not always headed towards open warfare. The contest between the superpowers eventually began to look more like a stalemate than a tug-of-war. Following the move by West Germany to engage the Soviet Union, the superpowers recognized that they had a common interest in maintaining peace. It was at this time, otherwise known as Détente, that the two superpowers, their allies, and non-aligned states in Europe came together to focus on security and cooperation.

In order to understand the nature of European security before and after the Final Act, we need to come to terms with the advent of the Cold War and its development over time. This chapter pays special attention to events such as the Berlin Airlift, the arms race, the founding of NATO, and the Cuban Missile Crisis.[1] In addition, we look at those European organizations that also engage European security and cooperation, and who are also relics of the Cold War. We look at the EU, NATO, and the Council of Europe specifically. As we discuss other European organizations, we need to bear in mind the question that we return to in Chapter 7: with the plethora of organizations in Europe today, does the OSCE continue to have a role in the European security architecture? Let us begin with a look at Europe in the post-war period.

From Cold War to Cold Peace

The First World War (1914–18) and the Second World War (1939–45), produced two factors that would change international politics. First, the wars quickened the decline of Europe's traditional imperial powers, Great Britain and France. At the same time, the wars pushed two new superpowers to the forefront, the United States and the Soviet Union. Second, with the rise of the new superpowers came the advent of the Cold War. Relations between the United States and the Soviet Union before the Second World War were not at their best. The US administration did not recognize the Soviet Union until 1933, just before the Soviet Union became a member of the inter-war organization, the League of Nations. When the United States and the Soviet Union became allies in the Second World War against Nazi Germany and nominally against Japan, the US administration was slow to extend the same privileges to the Soviet Union that it had done for its other allies. Thus, before and during the war, the relationship between the United States and the Soviet Union was cool at best.

However, the Cold War fully developed following the capitulation of Nazi Germany and the subsequent American and Soviet occupation of Europe. The United States and its allies maintained a presence in Western Europe, in the states that they had helped to liberate. Likewise, the Soviet Red Army dominated Central and Eastern Europe for much the same reason. Both superpowers facilitated the creation of regimes that would match well their own intents and purposes. Thus, Western Europe, with some exceptions such as Spain and Portugal, maintained or built liberal democratic regimes with a market economy. In Central and Eastern Europe, the Soviets helped produce authoritarian regimes with command economies. Both superpowers saw it as in their interest to influence regimes in the other's sphere of influence. This common foreign policy tactic would dominate international politics until the end of the Cold War in 1991, not only in Europe, but in the rest of the world as well.

Nowhere was the Cold War felt so acutely as in Germany. For the Soviet Union and many other states in Europe, a militarized Germany had brought about two world wars and millions of deaths. Following Germany's defeat, the country was split into four sectors: the United

States in the South, France in the West, Great Britain in the North, and the Soviet Union in the East. Likewise, Berlin was also split into four sectors despite lying deep within the eastern, Soviet sector. During the occupation, the US administration and the Soviet authorities diverged in their plans for Germany. The Soviets wanted heavy reparations from Germany, similar to what the French and British had seen in the Treaty of Versailles following the First World War. Furthermore, based on the conditions of the Potsdam Conference in 1945, the Soviets demanded that Germany be demilitarized. On the other hand, the Americans wanted a rebuilt Germany since the harsh conditions for Germany following the First World War were perceived as leading to the Second World War. Furthermore, the Americans wanted to maintain a German defense force to defend against a possible Soviet land invasion. Since the Americans, French, and British refused to seek war reparations, the Soviets declared their eastern sector a separate state and produced a communist government (East Germany). The Western allies responded by joining their three sectors into one unified state (West Germany).

On 24 June 1948, the Soviets began to block land access to the allied sectors in Berlin. Considering first an armored response to force the Soviets to open the East German borders, the US administration decided on 25 June to use an airlift to bring resources into the allied enclave. The Soviet blockade lasted until 12 May 1949. The Berlin Airlift had three effects on post-war international politics. First, the airlift helped galvanize the allied effort following a change in leadership in the Western allies. For example, during the Berlin Airlift, the Western allies signed the North Atlantic Treaty that established NATO. The treaty created an alliance designed to bring a defensive response to a Soviet invasion, should it come. Second, the Berlin Airlift helped guarantee that Germany would remain split between East and West until its reunification in 1990. Ironically, it would be West Germany's *rapprochement* with the Soviet Union that would bring about Détente. Finally, the Berlin Airlift confirmed the beginning of the Cold War as a contest between the Soviet Union and the United States and its allies. For Germany and especially Berlin, the Berlin Airlift began a division that would culminate in the Berlin Wall, created in 1961 to keep East Germans from fleeing to the West. Where the Berlin Airlift is often cited as the beginning of the Cold War, the collapse of the Berlin Wall in 1989 is likewise often cited as its end.

Germany once again had an impact on the Cold War when it joined NATO in 1955. In response, the Soviets and their allies came together under the Warsaw Treaty or Warsaw Pact to counter the perceived threat from NATO. The establishment of the Warsaw Pact in 1955 meant that the European security architecture was dominated by two opposing organizations representing each superpower. Like NATO, the Warsaw Pact was used to coordinate military exercises between signatories. However, unlike NATO, the Warsaw Pact was also used to reinforce Soviet domination in Central and Eastern Europe. Under the auspices of the Warsaw Pact, the Soviets invaded Hungary in 1956 and Czechoslovakia in 1967 when moderate, nationalist socialists came to power.

The contest between the East and West was made tense by the planned Soviet land invasion that never developed because of the perceived risk of a nuclear defense. Nuclear weapons meant the Cold War would have to remain "cold" since open conflict would mean mutually assured destruction (MAD). The United States had developed the nuclear bomb and used it in Japan in August 1945. The Soviet Union tested its first nuclear bomb in August 1949. As the delivery systems improved with advance of the space race, a war between the superpowers would have meant "total" war. While the Cold War was a global contest, the most likely place to set off a nuclear holocaust would have been the heavily militarized European continent. The United States and the Soviet Union used their treaty-based institutions to proliferate nuclear weapons in Europe, making for an ever increasing chance of conflict. As we know, nuclear war did not happen. Nor did the closest the world has ever come to nuclear war happen on the European landmass. It happened in Cuba.

Fidel Castro came to power in a socialist revolution in Cuba in 1959. The United States had been a close ally to the ousted Fulgencio Batista regime. Like much of the rest of Latin America, the United States had significant trade interests in Cuba. The United States had attempted to force Cuba back in the failed "Bay of Pigs" intervention in 1961. Subsequently, Castro declared Cuba to be a socialist state and sought support from Moscow. The Soviet authorities responded with resources such as aid and technical expertise. As alluded to earlier, the United States had placed nuclear weapons in other countries in Europe, but most importantly in Turkey who maintained a border with the Soviet Union. In 1962, the Soviets responded by placing nuclear weapons in Cuba, just off the coast of the United States. What followed is known as the Cuban Missile Crisis. US intelligence discovered the missiles in Cuba using surveillance flights. The US administration placed a naval blockade around Cuba and stated that it would fire on any ships that attempted to pass the blockade. As Soviet ships were progressing towards the blockade, the stage was set for a nuclear war. In order to remove the missiles from Cuba, the Soviet leader Nikita

Khrushchev asked in letters sent to the US President John F. Kennedy that the US government vow not to invade Cuba and to remove US missiles from Turkey. Nuclear war was averted when Kennedy accepted Khrushchev's deal. Unfortunately for the Soviet leader, the result meant that Khrushchev had little time left in office following the crisis. He was replaced by Leonid Brezhnev shortly afterwards. The stage was set for Détente.

Cold Peace and the spirit of Détente

The world narrowly avoided a nuclear war in 1962. The benefit was that US-Soviet diplomatic communications improved after the crisis. The Cold War was no less "cold" and no less a "war," but competition between the superpowers began to ebb as the Soviet Union had to deal with its own stagnating economy and the United States faced a never-ending war in Vietnam. The European security environment changed for the better. By this time, the current status quo in Europe was settled with the US and West German acceptance of the two German states. At the same time, the Soviets agreed to the current dividing line between East and West. The majority of states were either part of NATO or the Warsaw Pact, although there were notable exceptions such as Spain and Yugoslavia. Nevertheless, while the Cold War remained a violent ideological conflict in the developing world, a status quo regarding dividing lines in Europe was agreed between the superpowers. Thus, rather than a dynamic conflict, the Cold War in Europe was about policing the dividing line. In the early 1970s, US and Soviet foreign policies altered again to confirm the status quo. This change has been referred to as Détente. With the United States bogged down in Vietnam and the static politics of the Brezhnev regime in the Soviet Union, relations between superpowers became more communicative, if not more cooperative. It is during this phase that the CSCE was created.

Between the two superpowers, the Cold War had stabilized after the Cuban Missile Crisis. In the Soviet Union, the leadership transition that came with Stalin's death ended with the rise of Brezhnev (1964). The leadership contest was essentially over and the cadre system of the Brezhnev government meant that little changed in the echelons of Soviet leadership.[2] At the same time, the Soviet Union had improved its military capabilities to match those of the United States. Domestic political stability and a greater sense of military capacity led Soviet decision-makers to perceive the West as less of a threat. The United States, on the other hand, was embroiled in a conflict in Vietnam with little real chance of victory. The ferocious defense of the North Vietnamese Vietcong despite massive casualties meant that American victory was all but impossible. The "strategy of containment" led the United States to become involved in South Asia as it had done in Korea.[3] The loss (or the lack of victory) in Vietnam made the strategy of containment an unworkable foreign policy in its most explicit form. This is not to say that containment did not still dominate US national security strategies but rather overt military adventures would be replaced by covert support for pro-American regimes and opposition groups in the developing world.

The cooperation that led to the Helsinki Final Act is the high point of Détente in Europe.[4] The Final Act was the confirmation of the current power arrangement in Europe. West Germany's policy of *Ostpolitik* confirmed that the Soviet's traditional enemy, the German state, acknowledged the status quo and pledged diplomatic solutions to any future problems.[5] The policy allowed West Germany to improve relations with its immediate eastern neighbors, such as East Germany, Poland, and Czechoslovakia. With this change, Europe's focus moved away from "collective" security to "common and comprehensive" security.

With the ideals of the CSCE confirmed in the Helsinki Final Act, the spirit of the positive-sum game among the superpowers returned to confrontation. In 1979, the Soviet Union invaded Afghanistan in order to support a socialist regime that it had helped come to power. The United States and its allies condemned the invasion. Like the United States in Vietnam, the Soviet Union was waging a war against impossible odds. "Total war" would be the route to victory in Afghanistan, but like the United States in Vietnam, this was not part of the plan. Coupled with domestic insurgency against the Soviets, the United States fostered support through a network of Islamic fighters that as we now know present many of the challenges that face the OSCE region today. The election of Ronald Reagan (1980) in the United States also brought about a more confrontational American foreign policy. The Reagan administration chose to increase the rate of military development and acquisition as a means of outpacing the Soviet Union. With the death of Brezhnev in 1982 and the eventual rise to power of Mikhail Gorbachev in 1985, the Soviet Union and Central and Eastern Europe were ready for change. In 1989, the Eastern bloc began to collapse.

From the beginning, the CSCE was faced with numerous challenges. Coherence and decision-making were the main problems facing the CSCE. The Final Act was about promoting communication and cooperation. This fits with Robert Keohane's definition of an international organization as institutionalized political communication.[6] Through this process, the states of East and West would come together to preserve common security in the Euro-Atlantic area. As the end of the Cold War began to change the political dynamics of the CSCE region, the CSCE had a role to play in maintaining security and cooperation during this turbulent time. Predicated on mediating superpower politics, the CSCE began to focus on how to help transitioning states remain peaceful and stable. Yet, the CSCE was not the only organization aimed at maintaining peace and stability in the region but only one of several organizations that had an interest in facing the challenges brought about by the end of the Cold War.

The regional organizational infrastructure

The Euro-Atlantic area is organizationally heavily laden. There are several organizations that cover the region in addition to the OSCE, such as the EU, NATO, and the Council of Europe. At the same time, the majority of European states are members of several, if not all, of these organizations. For example, the United Kingdom is a member of them all. During the Cold War, each of these organizations had their role to play in the social, economic, and political dimensions of Europe. Yet, after the Cold War, the roles and responsibilities of these regional organizations begin to converge. As seen in Box 1.1, the OSCE has a large membership, incorporating NATO member-states, former Warsaw Pact member-states or their remnants, as well as the European neutral and formerly non-aligned states.

With the growing overlap in organizational membership, on one hand, as well as the converging paths of the organizations themselves, on the other, this book asks the following question: Does the OSCE remain a relevant organization today? The argument portrayed in the following chapters is that the OSCE has been and still remains an important organization for the Euro-Atlantic area. The conciliatory approach of the CSCE during the Cold War and the important Helsinki Final Act meant that the legacies of Détente have lasted much longer than Détente itself. Following the collapse of socialist regimes in Central and Eastern Europe and the Soviet Union, the OSCE has restructured itself to engage with the changing politics of the larger region. At the same time, other organizations have themselves experienced considerable change since the end of the Cold War, not only in membership but also in their roles and responsibilities in the region. A brief glance at the other regional organizations will allow us to put the OSCE into a regional and organizational context as well as engage with the question of contemporary relevance.

Box 1.1 Membership of the OSCE

Albania (1991)
Andorra (1996)
Armenia (1992)
Austria (1973)
Azerbaijan (1992)
Belarus (1992)
Belgium (1973)
Bosnia and Herzegovina (1992)
Bulgaria (1973)
Canada (1973)
Croatia (1992)
Cyprus (1973)
Czech Republic (1993)
Denmark (1973)
Estonia (1991)
Finland (1973)
Former Yugoslav Republic of
  Macedonia (1995)
Georgia (1992)
France (1973)
Germany (1973)
Greece (1973)
Holy See (1973)
Hungary (1973)
Iceland (1973)
Ireland (1973)
Italy (1973)
Kazakhstan (1992)
Kyrgyzstan (1992)

Latvia (1991)
Liechtenstein (1973)
Lithuania (1991)
Luxembourg (1973)
Malta (1973)
Moldova (1992)
Monaco (1973)
Montenegro (2006)
The Netherlands (1973)
Norway (1973)
Poland (1973)
Portugal (1973)
Romania (1973)
Russian Federation (1973 as
  the USSR)
San Marino (1973)
Serbia (2000)
Slovak Republic (1993)
Slovenia (1992)
Spain (1973)
Sweden (1973)
Switzerland (1973)
Tajikistan (1992)
Turkey (1973)
Turkmenistan (1992)
Ukraine (1992)
United Kingdom (1973)
United States of America (1973)
Uzbekistan (1992)

The European Union (EU)

The European Union that we see today has gone through significant changes from its origins in the Treaty of Paris. In fact, the EU is an amalgamation of three "communities." In 1951, the countries of France, West Germany, Italy, the Netherlands, Belgium, and Luxembourg signed the Treaty of Paris which set up the European Coal and Steel Community (ECSC), making pooling natural resources easier between the six countries. In 1957, the first Treaty of Rome established the European Economic Community, creating a common market between the six countries, while a second Treaty of Rome established the European Atomic Energy Community. Together, these two "communities" created in 1957 were known as the European Community. In 1965, the Merger Treaty brought the three "communities" together under one organizational umbrella. This treaty created the European Commission and the European Council. Until the 1980s, together the European Communities were focused on the economic agenda among the member-states. The agenda widened in 1986 with the Single European Act, which reformed the earlier 1957 treaties but also added a political dimension to the European Community. This reform momentum eventually led to the Maastricht Treaty (or Treaty of the European Union) in 1992 which created the EU, transferring the "communities" into "pillars."

The European Community did not remain an organization of only six states. Great Britain, Ireland, and Denmark became members in 1973, although they had originally applied in 1961. The 1973 enlargement was followed by Greece in 1981, as well as Spain and Portugal in 1986. Following the 1986 enlargement, the European Community went through a widening of its agenda to a political, as well as economic, organization. The political dimension came to be known as the Common Foreign and Security Policy (CFSP). The traditionally neutral states of Finland, Austria, and Sweden became members in 1995, following a change in foreign policies in the post-Cold War era. In 1995, the EU consisted of 15 member-states. Future enlargements would be a matter of CFSP. In fact, the enlargement process would become the largest CFSP initiative in the EU (Box 1.2).

In May 2004, the EU experienced its largest enlargement with ten new member-states, all of whom were also members of the OSCE. The EU has traditionally been an economic organization first, and a political and social organization second, with its key asset the common market. During the Cold War, the European Community helped bolster and support West European economies while at the same time guaranteeing friendly relations between France and West Germany. The assumption was that through complex interdependencies, relations between traditional enemies would be far less likely to degenerate into conflict.[7] The European Community helped foster these interdependencies. At the same time, the European Community "locked in" domestic political agents, groups, and institutions that would support liberal, democratic capitalism, again in an attempt to reduce the chances of another European conflict.[8]

Box 1.2 Membership of the European Union

Current member-states and date of entry

Austria (1995)	Lithuania (2004)
Belgium (1951)	Luxembourg (1951)
Cyprus (2004)	Malta (2004)
Czech Republic (2004)	The Netherlands (1951)
Denmark (1973)	Poland (2004)
Estonia (2004)	Portugal (1986)
Finland (1995)	Slovakia (2004)
France (1951)	Slovenia (2004)
Germany (1951)	Spain (1986)
Greece (1981)	Sweden (1995)
Hungary (2004)	United Kingdom (1973)
Ireland (1973)	Bulgaria (2007)
Italy (1951)	Romania (2007)
Latvia (2004)	

In membership negotiations

Croatia
Turkey

With each enlargement, the EU has evolved to become not only a major economic actor, but also a political and social organization as well. For the latest EU enlargement, accession states were required to meet the so-called *Copenhagen Criteria* as developed in the 1993 Copenhagen European Council. These are:

- stability of institutions guaranteeing democracy, the rule of law, human rights, and respect for and protection of minorities;
- the existence of a functioning market economy as well as the capacity to cope with competitive pressure and market forces within the Union;
- the ability to take on the obligations of membership including adherence to the aims of political, economic and monetary union.

In the criteria, as we will see, there is a great deal of overlap with the OSCE and the Council of Europe. The EU's influence also reaches beyond the borders of the EU. Considerable attention has been paid in the EU to the former Soviet area (excluding the Baltic States) through the Northern Dimension Initiative and the "Wider Europe-Neighbourhood" framework, otherwise known as the European Neighbourhood Policy. Finally, with EU peacekeepers in the former Yugoslavia, the EU has increasingly taken on the role of peace operations in the region. Is this encroachment on the OSCE, a strengthening of its core principles through other organizations, or simply a complementary addition to the European security architecture?

The North Atlantic Treaty Organization (NATO)

As discussed earlier, NATO was created in the midst of the Berlin Airlift in 1949. Before the founding of the North Atlantic Treaty Organization, the West European states had come together in the West European Defence Organization in 1948. This organization did not include the United States, mostly because US legislation barred entering into any formal alliances. However, in 1948 the so-called Vandenburg Resolution allowed the United States to enter into an Atlantic alliance. NATO was established to be a collective defense organization against a possible land invasion by the Soviet Union. Article V of the North Atlantic Treaty mandates that should a member-state be attacked, other member-states must come to their aid militarily. NATO had six primary responsibilities in the Cold War. First, the alliance was established to balance Soviet power in Europe. Second, together the member-states of NATO could ensure a retaliatory strike on any Soviet attack. Third, the member-states of NATO worked together to gather intelligence on the Soviet Union. Fourth, NATO monitored the borders between member-states and Central and Eastern Europe. It is important to note that NATO had a border with the Soviet Union from the outset with Norway's northern frontier. Fifth, NATO was able to monitor any Soviet incursions, either on land, by sea, or by air. Finally, the organization existed to deter any Soviet opportunity for attack. While deterrence is difficult to show, there is little doubt that the coordination between the North Atlantic Treaty states did have an impact on the Soviet cost-benefit perception as to whether or not to attack.

Today, NATO remains a traditional security alliance although we have seen considerable changes since the end of the Cold War. During the Cold War, NATO was simply one of two opposing blocs (the other being the Warsaw Pact) whose members also became part of the CSCE. Where the OSCE is a political organization, NATO by all accounts is a military organization. However, there are significant

Box 1.3 Membership of NATO and partner states

Member states	Partner states
Belgium (1949)	Albania
Bulgaria (2004)	Armenia
Canada (1949)	Austria
Czech Republic (1999)	Azerbaijan
Denmark (1949)	Belarus
Estonia (2004)	Croatia
France (1949)	Cyprus
Germany (1955 as West	Finland
Germany)	Former Yugoslav Republic of
Greece (1952)	Macedonia
Hungary (1999)	Georgia
Iceland (1949)	Kazakhstan
Italy (1949)	Kyrgyzstan
Latvia (2004)	Malta
Lithuania (2004)	Moldova
Luxembourg (1949)	Republic of Ireland
Netherlands (1949)	Russian Federation
Norway (1949)	Sweden
Poland (1999)	Switzerland
Portugal (1949)	Tajikistan
Romania (2004)	Turkmenistan
Slovakia (2004)	Ukraine
Slovenia (2004)	Uzbekistan
Spain (1982)	
Turkey (1952)	
United Kingdom (1949)	
United States (1949)	

overlaps at least in terms of themes that both the OSCE and NATO address: security and cooperation. Traditionally, NATO has been limited to collective defense, which limits the organization to its own borders. But with the 1999 and 2004 enlargements, on one hand, and the development of "out-of-area operations," on the other, we have seen NATO's thematic and geographic responsibilities develop to increasingly overlap with those of the OSCE.

Following changes in Central and Eastern Europe, NATO immediately began to change as an organization in order to counter the new threats to European security. In 1990, the London Declaration refocused the alliance's attention away from the Soviet Union and thus collective defense towards the breakdown of stable states and collective security. NATO's engagement with the former Eastern bloc was further enhanced in 1994 with the Partnership for Peace (PfP) program. PfP set out to further the aim of collective security by developing cooperation between NATO and non-member-states, including those in the former Soviet space. For some states, PfP was a training ground for prospective enlargement while others (e.g. Russia) saw it as a way to moderate NATO to its own ends.[9] Box 1.3 lists both NATO members and the current PfP states. With the attacks on the World Trade Center in New York in 2001, NATO once again changed to establish a policy of out-of-area operations in the 2002 Prague North Atlantic Council. This aim was once again reaffirmed in 2004 in the Istanbul North Atlantic Council which focused specifically on operations in the Caucuses and Central Asia. Where before, the OSCE had been the only Euro-Atlantic organization involved in the region, NATO stepped in to press on with the "War on Terror." As a security organization, NATO has the capacity to be a much more effective assurer of peace and stability in the region. The question remains in relation to NATO, what is the role for the OSCE in assuring peace and cooperation in the Euro-Atlantic area?

The Council of Europe

Europe's democratic credentials are arguably best personified in the Council of Europe (Box 1.4). Created in 1949, the council pre-dates the other three organizations. Like the later European Coal and Steel Community, the key purpose of the council was to facilitate political communication throughout Europe. At the core of the council from the beginning was support for liberal democracy and human rights. Furthermore, the purpose of the council was to help develop a "European" identity that would help suppress the nationalist roots of conflict in the First and Second World Wars. Much like the OSCE today, the council was soon contending for attention among a plethora of new regional and international organizations. However, the council's attention to democracy and human rights set it apart from the other organizations, not to mention its specifically European membership.

The Council of Europe's role in Europe after the end of the Cold War is similar to that of the OSCE. Three characteristics present themselves. First, the council became the region's principal human rights guarantor. In 1959, the council created the European Court of Human Rights to be followed with the creation of the Commissioner on Human Rights in 1999. Second, like the OSCE, the council played an important role in European integration and enlargement. The council's Framework Convention for the Protection of National Minorities has become an accepted standard for minority protection in Central and Eastern Europe. Finally, the council has been a repository of "best practices" to common problems, such as illegal immigration, organized crime, and human trafficking. While the Council of Europe is not a security organization, the securitization of democracy and human rights in Central and Eastern Europe, as the conflict in the former Yugoslavia illustrates, has led towards a greater convergence of interests with the EU, NATO, and the OSCE.

Box 1.4 Membership of the Council of Europe

Albania (1995)	Latvia (1995)
Andorra (1994)	Liechtenstein (1978)
Armenia (2001)	Lithuania (1993)
Austria (1956)	Luxembourg (1949)
Azerbaijan (2001)	Malta (1965)
Belgium (1949)	Moldova (1995)
Bosnia and Herzegovina (2002)	Monaco (2004)
Bulgaria (1992)	Montenegro (2006)
Croatia (1996)	The Netherlands (1949)
Cyprus (1961)	Norway (1949)
Czech Republic (1993)	Poland (1991)
Denmark (1949)	Portugal (1976)
Estonia (1993)	Romania (1993)
Finland (1989)	Russian Federation (1996)
Former Yugoslav Republic of Macedonia (1995)	San Marino (1988)
	Serbia (2003)
France (1949)	Slovakia (1993)
Georgia (1999)	Slovenia (1993)
Germany (1950)	Spain (1977)
Greece (1949)	Sweden (1949)
Hungary (1990)	Switzerland (1963)
Iceland (1950)	Turkey (1949)
Ireland (1949)	Ukraine (1995)
Italy (1949)	United Kingdom (1949)

Conclusion

As mentioned, the fabric of organizations in Europe is particularly thick. No other region has such a dense network of organizations that deal with the political, economic, and the social. NATO began as a way to balance Soviet hegemony in Europe and has now transitioned into a collective security organization with a series of "out-of-area" operations in the Balkans and Afghanistan. The EU began as an economic organization that, although it was never far from the political, did not become explicitly thus until the Single European Act in 1986. Finally, the Council of Europe has seen the least change in its aims and objectives since it set out in 1949. The Council of Europe remains engaged with the promotion of democracy and human rights in Europe. Whether the North Atlantic Treaty, the Treaty of Paris, or the Council of Europe's founding Treaty of London, all of these organizations are different from the CSCE/OSCE in that they are based on legal commitments. As we shall see in the next chapter, the Helsinki Final Act avoided legal obligations in favor of political commitments.

Finally, the European security architecture that existed when the CSCE was created was dominated by the Cold War. The United States and Soviet Union went from being reluctant allies in the Second World War to become enemies in the post-war arrangement. The United States and its allies perceived the Soviets as having imperial ambitions on the European continent. There is very little evidence that this was not the case. On the part of the Soviet Union, leaders in Moscow perceived the United States and West Germany as a threat to their survival. Likewise, the evidence shows that the United States was keen to break the power of the Soviets regionally and globally. Nevertheless, the Cold War turned to Cold Peace following the Cuban Missile Crisis, the rise to power of Brezhnev in the Soviet Union, and the *Ostpolitik* foreign policy of West Germany. The era of Détente provided Europe with an opportunity to seek stability, peace, and cooperation in Europe. As we will see in Chapter 2, the CSCE was the fruit of Détente.

2 The Helsinki Final Act and comprehensive security

Optimism in the Euro-Atlantic area has come about twice in the past 35 years. The most recent was at the end of the Cold War. The great divide between East and West was no longer. The world had stepped back from nuclear obliteration. However, the first occurrence was important but not nearly so grand. This was the series of agreements in 1975 that led to the Helsinki Final Act and the creation of the Conference on Security and Cooperation in Europe (CSCE). The Final Act froze the current status quo in the Euro-Atlantic area. Borders would not be challenged, national sovereignty would be strengthened, and confidence- and security-building measures would encourage an environment of peace and cooperation. With the dominance of the two superpowers playing Cold War politics, the Final Act is the best that we could have expected in 1975 and arguably until the fall of the Berlin Wall and the dissolution of the Soviet Union. The Final Act improved the environment of the Euro-Atlantic area, but the document did not fundamentally change it.

Nevertheless, the Final Act has become an important document for three reasons. First, the Final Act foreshadowed the end of the Cold War. Cooperation, at least on some level, was possible. The Final Act also established the aims and objectives that would be needed to preserve security and cooperation in the Euro-Atlantic area as the Soviet Union collapsed and the Americans withdrew. Second, the Final Act was the first international agreement which set out a comprehensive, holistic approach to security. The focus on varied dimensions of security is astonishing considering the overwhelming threat of transitional, strategic (in)securities. The CSCE was predicated on addressing three dimensions of security: (1) politico-military security; (2) economic and environmental security; and (3) human security. Much of the academic debate since has been on broadening the security agenda to take in alternatives to traditional security concerns. The Final Act was ahead of its time. Finally, the Final Act made the CSCE and thus the OSCE a very different type of international organization. Where the UN, the Council of Europe, and other treaty-based organizations have their foundations in *legal* commitments, the OSCE is based on *political* commitments. The political nature of the OSCE has been both an asset and a burden, as we shall see.[1] Nevertheless, this makes the OSCE a different sort of organization to others, with different mechanisms with which to address threats to security and cooperation.

This chapter is divided into three sections. We take a look at the path to the Helsinki negotiations which created the Final Act and the CSCE. In particular, we look at the changing climate of the Cold War which led to agreement and cooperation. The second section discusses the Final Act in depth and the politics behind it. We also look at the different dimensions of security enshrined in the Final Act. The final section looks at the legacy of the Final Act. In particular, this chapter argues that the Final Act has shaped international law, European integration, and the human rights discourse, as well as our conceptualization of security. For these reasons, the Final Act is worth investigating further and introduces us to the basic principles, aims, and objectives of the current OSCE.

The path to Helsinki

The Cold War was a period of superpower politics. The nature of Cold War international politics was "balance or bandwagon." Some states could extract themselves from the power struggle, but few did so successfully. For instance, Finnish foreign policy following the Second World War was based on constructive neutrality, especially *vis-à-vis* the Soviet Union.[2] However, there is very little room for outsiders in a zero-sum international system. Pekka Sivonen points out that the Cold War itself only lasted from 1946–47 to 1963, but the Cold War system lasted much longer.[3] Following the Cuban Missile Crisis, the two superpowers began to open up lines of communication to ensure peace and stability, if not exactly cooperation. The "warmer" parts of the Cold War were being fought in proxy wars in Asia, Africa, and Latin America, leaving the Cold War in Europe a stalemate between the East and West, otherwise known as the "long peace."[4]

The Soviets began to seek a confirmation of the Cold War system as it existed in Europe in the 1950s.[5] Following the end of the war, the Soviet Union continued to occupy the Baltic Republics and maintain a threat of military force in Central and Eastern Europe, even using force to quell "drifters" in Hungary and Czechoslovakia. The Soviets also saw a divided Germany as an assurance that it would not rise again. In essence, the Soviet government sought a confirmation of Cold War borders. The US policy towards the Soviet Union during the Cold War was containment.[6] Containment was a policy of restricting the extension of Soviet domination. Yet, containment was also a policy of confirming the status quo. US policy-makers were keen to put out the fires of international socialism around the world. At the same time, the United States was in no position to restructure the Cold War in Europe, especially since the Soviets had their own arsenal of nuclear weapons.[7] Thus, by default, the Soviets and Americans were reading from the same script although from opposite sides.

Two "Declarations" laid the path to Helsinki. The culmination of Soviet policy came when the countries of the Warsaw Pact set out an agenda of communication between East and West in the 1966 Bucharest Declaration.[8] The Declaration called for a conference to discuss conflict and security between the European countries (i.e. not the United States or Canada). The purpose of the conference would be two-fold. First, the goal would be to confirm current European borders. Second, the conference would be aimed at promoting cooperation between European countries in the areas of science, technology, and culture, something already done in Western Europe by the Council of Europe.[9] The West responded in 1969 with the Declaration on European Security, which to some degree complemented the Warsaw Pact Declaration. NATO added to the topics to be discussed including the environment and what would be known as the "human dimension" of the CSCE. Russell argues that the NATO Declaration established a process of informal dialogue between East and West. This dialogue eventually led to the Helsinki Process.[10]

Soviet and American discussions on future regional cooperation in general and military forces in Europe specifically began in 1972 with US President Richard Nixon's visit to Moscow to discuss a proposed conference and the Mutual and Balanced Force Reduction talks.[11] The Cold War dialogue had moved up a gear. In particular, the status of the two German states illustrated the progress of Détente. In 1973, West Germany gained UN membership. By 1974, the United States had recognized East Germany and begun full diplomatic operations. As discussed in Chapter 1, both Germanies played an important part as *actors* in influencing closer relations between East and West. Not only did West Germany initiate *Ostpolitik* to engage the Soviet Union, but also the East and West German states were key *subjects* of Détente. The nature of the Cold War in Europe had clearly changed.

Europe needed a rule book to spell out the new rules of engagement and arguably, a regime to make sure that participants were playing by the rules. Such rules would be discussed in a conference that would eventually include not only European states but also the United States and Canada.

The final act

The Helsinki Final Act was in fact the end product of an extended negotiation that lasted for two years. The Helsinki Process consisted of three stages, beginning in September 1972. The first stage lasted nearly nine months and produced the "Final Recommendations of the Helsinki Consultation." The second stage took place (in Geneva) from September 1973 to July 1975. Stage two produced the "Final Act" which was signed at stage three in Helsinki on 1 August 1975. The Final Act is in fact the product of a long process of bargaining between five categories of actors. First, the most stalwart Warsaw Pact states, including the Soviet Union, had been supportive of a conference since the Warsaw Pact Bucharest Declaration in 1966. The second group included those Warsaw Pact states that were rather wary of Soviet dominance in the region, including Hungary, Romania, and Czechoslovakia. The third group included neutral states such as Ireland, Sweden, and Switzerland who were particularly keen to keep the Final Act from encroaching on their neutrality. Fourth, the countries of the European Community often worked together on a unified front in the negotiations.[12] Finally, the most stalwart states of NATO, in particular the United States, attempted to use the Helsinki Process not simply to accept the status quo, but also to set in place mechanisms for change. Although a member of the EC since 1973, the UK fits more neatly in the final category. This scheme is a simplified categorization of the actors in the Helsinki Process but still offers a way to observe similar actors who held similar perspectives and objectives.[13]

There is a paucity of literature on the bargaining that went on between participating states of the conference. We need an observer of the negotiations to get a clear idea of the actors and the route of the bargaining process. Delegates are naturally subjective, but they nevertheless offer an insight into negotiations. The nearest we can come to such an observer is Harold S. Russell from the US delegation to the CSCE negotiations who reported on the process, asking the question of the Final Act, "Brobdingnag or Lilliput?" alluding to Jonathan Swift's story *Gulliver's Travels*.[14] Russell was responding to the media indifference and the political criticism of the resulting Final Act. In particular, the Final Act was perceived as a victory for the Soviets since it confirmed one of their long-held foreign policy objectives: "recognizing Soviet post-war hegemony in Eastern Europe without any substantial *quid pro quo.*"[15] Russell highlights the political nature of the CSCE negotiations. In particular, he points out that virtually every participating state wanted the resulting document to be morally compelling but not legally binding. Interestingly, the UK put forward the notion of a "Final Act" to bring the conference to a close, which was subsequently adopted by the European Community.[16] There appeared a split between those who wanted the Final Act to be more or less binding. The first group of actors, including the Soviet Union, was keen to see the Final Act put forward as a morally compelling document, though remain not legal in nature, while the fifth group, including the United States and the UK, supported a proposal to include text in the Final Act to state that it was not a treaty or international agreement. The final solution was something in between. Russell writes:

> the [Final Act], then, is not a legal document and does not purport to state international law. It is viewed, however, as consistent with international law, and, given the level at which it was concluded, many observers think it may become in fact one of the most widely quoted sources of *customary international law.*[17]

This quote from Russell illustrates the close relationship that the Final Act has with international law without the document being legal in its own right. This moral-political basis of the OSCE remains one of its defining features.

As suggested, the Final Act was a confirmation by the West of the Soviet hegemony in Central and Eastern Europe. What was most important from the Soviet perspective is that the European status quo was confirmed. The USA in particular wanted to limit Soviet occupation (in some cases) and external control (in other cases) that had come about with the post-war settlement. Ultimately for the United States, the Final Act meant a policy of "containment without confrontation."[18] The Warsaw Pact countries and some of the neutral states such as Yugoslavia wanted an assurance that the Soviets would be less likely to violate state sovereignty as it had done in Hungary and Czechoslovakia. Other neutral states wanted to make sure that the Final Act did not commit them to actions that would violate their policy of neutrality. Nevertheless, all the actors were most concerned with stepping down from the confrontation that could have ended in conflict on the European continent.

The negotiation of the Final Act was in fact a negotiation over semantics. Each participant was trying to extract as much from the negotiations as possible, as we should expect from participating nation-states. Russell reports how the Soviets invested considerable effort in attempting to avoid a clause that would prohibit using the Red Army as part of foreign policy within the Warsaw Pact.[19] This attempt by the Soviets was most evident in the negotiation over the clause discussing the "inviolability of frontiers," which they had insisted would be separate from a clause prohibiting the use of force. The Soviets were in something of a quandary. They wanted the West to accept the current borders but if they brought in a clause that preserved state boundaries could it contradict Soviet methods of control. So the trouble was trying to find a word that would suit the Soviet wish to justify its hegemony of Central and Eastern Europe, while the West wanted a word that would prohibit the Soviet's using force to maintain the current borders and political regimes. Eventually, the Soviet delegation was willing to accept nearly any English word as long as the Russian version could use the Russian *posiagat* (to encroach).[20] Versions of the Final Act in other languages could use the rather more descriptive word "assaulting." The Soviet willingness to use a separate word in the Russian version illustrates that there were two audiences, one international and one domestic, or what Robert Putnam refers to as "the logic of two-level games."[21] Nevertheless, it would have been naïve on the part of the other participants to expect that the Soviets would be restricted by the Final Act even where a difference in translation would seem to suggest otherwise.

As Box 2.1 illustrates, the Final Act established three areas of concern for the CSCE. These are the three "baskets" of the Final Act and at the same time are the three "dimensions" of the CSCE. Basket I deals with politico-military relations and confidence- and security-building measures (CSBMs). Basket II relates to the economic and environmental dimension, which includes promoting economic development and environmental cooperation. Basket III focuses on the exchange of culture, science technology and the universality of human rights. Although the three dimensions do not fully come into their own until after the Cold War, we will look at each in turn as discussed in the Final Act. Let us first move on to discuss the ten core principles as presented in the "Decalogue."

The so-called "Decalogue" that was presented in Section 1(a) of the Final Act lists the priorities of the CSCE. Six of the ten principles directly relate to the politico-military dimension. Taken on its own, the Decalogue seems to set out overlapping principles, as we can see in

Box 2.1 The Helsinki Final Act

The three "Baskets" of the OSCE

I *Politico-Military Dimension*: concerns national sovereignty and the promotion of confidence- and security-building measures (CSBMs).
II *Economic-Environmental Dimension*: concerns regional cooperation in areas related to promoting economic development and combating environmental degradation.
III *Human Dimension*: concerns the universality of human rights through democratic processes and institutions.

The Helsinki Decalogue

1 Sovereign Equality, Respect for the Rights Inherent in Sovereignty
2 Refraining from the Threat or Use of Force
3 Inviolability of Frontiers
4 Territorial Integrity of States
5 Peaceful Settlement of Disputes
6 Non-Intervention in Internal Affairs
7 Respect for Human Rights and Fundamental Freedoms including the Freedom of Thought, Conscience, Religion or Belief
8 Equal Rights and Self-Determination of Peoples
9 Co-operation among States
10 Fulfilment in Good Faith of Obligations under International Law

Source: CSCE Final Act 1975 (www.osce.org/item/4046.html).

Box 2.1. For instance, protecting national sovereignty, the inviolability of frontiers and non-intervention are largely similar in nature. However, the politics behind the negotiations within the context of the Cold War offer us an explanation as to why these apparent redundancies are in the Decalogue. Russell argues that the Soviet delegation pushed strongly for these otherwise indivisible principles to be addressed separately.[22] The Soviet strategy was one way to deal with the conundrum in which they had found themselves. The aim was to guarantee the post-war border status quo while allowing for continued dominance in Central and Eastern Europe. In other words, it is difficult to ask others not to interfere while at the same time maintaining your own right to do so. Thus, the Soviets attempted to manipulate the negotiations to formalize this double standard by separating these otherwise indivisible principles. Let us look at each in more detail.

The first principle deals specifically with the right of states to maintain their national sovereignty, otherwise a reiteration of the Westphalian state-system. The Final Act states under this principle that states will respect "the rights of every State to judicial equality, to territorial integrity and to freedom and political independence."[23] With this, the Conference established the CSCE on the core principle of the UN Charter, national sovereignty. The principle of national sovereignty had a direct impact on the negotiation of the human dimension at the Conference. In particular, the Soviet delegation wanted to use the first principle to insist that Basket III be subject to each state's laws rather than be beholden to any international normative agenda.[24] As evidence, the text of the first principle finishes with a sentence that says that each state has the right to "choose and develop its political, social, economic, and cultural systems as well as its right to determine its laws and regulations."[25] Yet despite this, the West resisted the Soviet attempt to undermine the moral implications of the CSCE. The solution is what was termed the "Finnish compromise," because of the cooperation between the Soviet Union and Finland at the negotiations. The compromise was that Basket III would include a sentence saying that each participating state is morally obliged to adhere to the norms as they are set out in the Final Act, in addition to commitment of international law.

The second principle dealt with the threat and use of force. The negotiations were made more difficult by two outstanding confrontations.[26] First, the Soviet Union had seen it in its national interest to use force to quell rebellions in the Warsaw Pact countries. The threat of force to maintain socialist regimes was the basis of the Brezhnev Doctrine. The Soviet Union thus did not want to employ language that would preclude the use of force outright. Second, Turkey, and Greece (incidentally, both NATO members) were also aware of the implications for the conflict over Cyprus. For all four actors, the tension was in the word "pretext." For instance, Greece was keen to cause Turkey embarrassment by illustrating what it perceived to be the latter's use of a pretext for invading Cyprus. Turkey, on the other hand, believed that the invasion had been a response to an earlier bilateral agreement and had not invented a pretext. Thus, both the Soviet Union and Turkey did not want the word "pretext" employed. In the end, the result was an awkward phrasing that insisted on refraining from the threat or use of force. The problem, however, was not only confined to this principle.

The "inviolability of frontiers" principle was especially hard fought between delegations. The greatest amount of public attention was directed toward this principle. Interestingly, this principle is the briefest of the ten, comprising only two sentences. However, Russell says that the negotiation over these two sentences took four months of the nine-month Stage 2.[27] Again, as we discussed before, the problem was largely semantic which depended on whether the operative word would imply a use of force or not. The West wanted to use a word that explicitly suggested violation of borders by the use of force, while the Soviets wanted an open word that would include non-violent actions as well. The Soviets were keen to have the West accept the current borders and agree not to violate this arrangement through force or otherwise. In the end, participating states would interpret the third principle in whatever way suited their own interests.

The fourth "territorial integrity" principle was tied up with the "national sovereignty" and "inviolability of frontiers" principles. As stated, the Soviet delegation was keen to keep the issues separate for the purpose of justifying the status quo while allowing the Soviet government to continue a policy of prospective intervention. The fourth principle pertains to violations of territorial integrity by force or otherwise. Many Western and neutral participating delegations were keen to see the Final Act include a statement about potential transnational violations, such as environmental disasters.[28] The principle was also interpreted by some multi-ethnic states such as Yugoslavia to justify methods of inter-ethnic management. For this reason, it was believed by some that international efforts to address perceived discrimination and potential ethnic conflict would be sidelined. In other words, the human dimension would be restricted by the fourth principle. The principle also includes discussion on precluding territorial occupation. The Soviet delegation was happy to allow the Final Act to have a clause against occupation since the forceful inclusion of the Baltic Republics into the Soviet Union had been prior to the Final Act. Russell argues, however, that Western delegations saw this principle as de-legitimating not only future occupations, but also those that have already occurred.[29] Of special interest to the United States in particular was not to allow the Final Act to become a write-off of the Baltic Republics' claims to independence. Most recently, the Russian government has used the CSCE Final Act in an effort to justify its current border disputes with Estonia and Latvia, arguing that the "national sovereignty" and "territorial integrity" principles set the borders between the Russian SFSR and the Estonian SSR and Latvian SSR.[30]

The fifth principle is the "peaceful settlement of disputes," which Russell refers to as "the most disappointing and innocuous of the lot, in that it repeats the basic concepts of peaceful settlement of disputes as drawn from the UN Charter and strikes little new ground."[31] Indeed, the text offers little in a guide to peaceful settlements, simply calling on states to "endeavor in good faith and a spirit of cooperation" to reach a peaceful solution. However, how much progressive and innovative depth should we expect from the Final Act's introductory principles? Russell argues that the Italian delegation was particularly disappointed in the lack of an institutionalized mechanism that would have offered states a way to resolve disagreement peacefully. However, the Eastern bloc perceived an imposed restraint on the use of force if necessary as a violation of national sovereignty (principle one). Nevertheless, as we will see in the next chapter, as vague as the fifth principle may be, institutionalized mechanisms for conflict prevention and peace-making would eventually come about in the post-Cold War evolution of the CSCE.

Sixth, the Final Act calls on states to respect "non-intervention in internal affairs." The sixth principle again overlaps considerably with those discussed earlier. In the text, we can see that intervention is portrayed as the use of force or coercion, rather than more subtle means of interference. Russell argues that the West wanted a strong principle of non-intervention that would relegate the Brezhnev Doctrine to history, while at the same time allowing room for the human dimension to remain an important part of the CSCE.[32] Indeed, this balance is the reason we do see a focus on intervention as coercion. We would have expected some support from those states that had been victims of Soviet invasion in the Eastern Bloc, but yet outright opposition by the Soviet Union. Interestingly, Russell does not tell us of the Soviet position in the negotiation. The politics of Détente leading to the CSCE negotiations indicate that the Soviet government was willing to sacrifice the threat of intervention for the sake of Western acceptance of the current borders. Overall, Russell argues that the Soviets could have framed intervention in terms of protecting their own national sovereignty despite the Final Act.[33] The Soviet Union was also able to use bilateral treaties to ensure that the Brezhnev Doctrine remained a valid foreign policy. Nevertheless, the Soviet Union could not have used forceful intervention in the CSCE without violating the principles of the Final Act, regardless of framing.

While the first six principles in some way address coercive actions on other states, the remaining principles are less focused on inter-state conflict. Principle seven calls for the "respect for human rights and fundamental freedoms, including the freedom of thought conscience, religion or belief." Russell argues that this principle is the most innovative in the Final Act.[34] For instance, sovereignty, the inviolability of frontiers, and non-intervention are traditional principles of the Westphalian state-system. A principle addressing human rights it is not. The Soviets knew that a conference on security and cooperation in the region must address human rights. To this end, the Soviets went along but with the caveat that principle seven had to be based on the UN International Covenant on Civil and Political Rights (1966, but came into force 1976), which the Soviet Union had already recognized. The Covenant allows for states to restrict rights when they impede on the rights of others.[35] The role of the Soviet delegation was to limit the innovation of the human rights principle. Notwithstanding, principle seven has become one of the most important of the post-Cold War era, as we shall see in the forthcoming chapters.

The "equal rights and self-determination of peoples" principle is the last principle of substance. Russell's discussion of this principle is perhaps where we gain the clearest sense of his subjective analysis. For instance, he comments that "applying this concept to Europe says a great deal about the inability of some states in Europe to determine their own internal and external political, economic, social, and cultural systems," apparently without regard to his own country's mismanagement of minorities over time.[36] Nevertheless, the impact of national minorities in Europe on war and peace was important to the delegations and remains important for the OSCE.[37] Self-determination had ordinarily been aimed at decolonization, of which the United States and Soviet Union were prime instigators. Like principle seven, there is a tension here between the integrity of the state and the rights of individuals or groups, the same tension that exists in the UN Charter. States with significant, geographically concentrated national minorities were reluctant to see an open call for self-determination. In the end, the principle stated that the right to self-determination had to remain relevant to international norms of national sovereignty and integrity. Principle eight does little more than the international mechanisms to which it refers. However, the focus on minorities in particular would be the cornerstone of the human dimension and would eventually lead to the creation of a high commissioner on national minorities.

The final principles call for "cooperation among states" and "the fulfillment in good faith of obligations under international law." Both of the principles fit within the general spirit of the Final Act and a rhetorical basis for the cooperation that exists across the three dimensions of the CSCE. Nevertheless, it is fair to point out here that good relations between East and West did not develop. Détente was a limited period in the relationship between the Socialist bloc and the Western allies.[38] Yet, the Decalogue illustrates hard-fought bargaining on all sides. The Soviets were keen to make the West accept the post-war European architecture. The West was keen to make the Soviets capitulate on issues involving the principles of non-intervention and human rights. However, the most important aspect of the Final Act was its ability to make the Cold War more transparent. By looking at the three dimensions in more detail, we can build a picture of security and cooperation.

The three baskets

Basket I of the Final Act is the politico-military dimension, which is aimed at CSBMs. In this case, the Final Act was a follow-up of the 1973 Mutual and Balanced Force Reduction Talks (MBFR). In general, the Final Act establishes four methods to promote confidence and security. First, *notification* offers information to participating states regarding military maneuvers and movements. For instance, the Final Act dictates that major military maneuvers exceeding 25,000 troops (whether land, air or amphibious) will be reported 21 days or more in advance through "usual diplomatic channels." The phrase "usual diplomatic channels" perhaps illustrates the lack of institutions in the early CSCE. Second, CSBMs are based on *observation*.[39] Participating states are requested to invite other participating states to observe military maneuvers on a bilateral basis. Again, the focus here is on inter-governmental relationships rather than the CSCE as a third party. Furthermore, each government is allowed to dictate how many and under what conditions observers could be present. Third, in the spirit of the MBFR, the Final Act focuses on *disarmament* efforts "which are designed to complement political détente in Europe." Eventually, the Strategic Arms Reduction Treaty (START I) meetings in 1982 and the Conventional Forces in Europe (CFE) Treaty in 1992 would go further in regulating disarmament. The Final Act only offers a rhetorical argument for disarmament. Finally, Basket I works through promoting a spirit of *transparency*, an inherent part of a confidence-building objective. Transparency would eventually be a greater part of the East–West relationship as the Cold War drew to a close. Yet 1975 was a long way from the end of the Cold War.

While Basket I offers several specific programs for enhancing CSBMs, Basket II is far less focused.[40] It focuses on economic and environmental exchange, based on an assumed direct link between peace and security in the region. Overall, this basket has five components. First, the Final Act promotes "commercial exchanges," primarily through reducing barriers to trade. This also includes information exchange especially between large industries. Second, Basket II includes "industrial cooperation and projects of common interest." Again, there is little in the details other than a general recommendation to enhance cooperation. Third, there are "provisions concerning trade and industrial cooperation." These provisions focus on harmonization, arbitration and more specifically issues of double taxation. Fourth, Basket II includes a focus on "science and technology," which includes several fields of cooperation, including agriculture, energy, space research and medicine. Finally, the "environment" is addressed in Basket II. Particular attention is paid to pollution that has a transnational character such as air and water. Of Basket II, the environment section is the most constructive, instrumental and specific in its directives. For instance, Basket II is tied to several prior agreements such as the Stockholm Declaration on the Human Environment and other UN resolutions. Other than the environment section, Basket II offers little other than a rhetorical justification for general economic cooperation. While laudable, the Final Act fails to offer a guide that projects the future of the region particularly in the field of economic cooperation. Nor does it pertain to what is otherwise known as "economic security."[41] The failure of the current OSCE to focus on the economic-environmental dimension is a direct result of the lack of depth in Basket II. Furthermore, the challenge to the OSCE in this regard is related to the predominance of other international organizations in the field of economic cooperation (i.e. the EU).

Since the end of the Cold War, the human dimension, as it originates in Basket III, has focused primarily on democratization and human rights. However, Basket III, as it is defined in the Final Act, offers very little focus on democratization, although it does broadly address human rights. Primarily, Basket III is focused on familial, cultural and social exchanges. In the Final Act, Basket III addresses four specific areas. The first area is "human contacts." This is a belated attempt to reunite families that had been separated by migrations and borders in the early twentieth century. The Final Act calls on participating states to support the Red Cross and the Red Crescent in this regard. The first area also addresses marriages between citizens of different states as well as the promotion of exchanges between young people and sport.

The second area in Basket III is the exchange of information, such as print matter and films. Furthermore, by concentrating on the working conditions of journalists, the second area establishes the basis for the OSCE Representative on Freedom of the Media created in 1997. Third, and in this context, the Final Act also addresses "cooperation and exchanges in the field of culture." There is particular focus on the exchange of the arts and literature between participating states. The final area is "cooperation and exchanges in the field of education." The Final Act concentrates on student and teacher exchanges, collaboration in science, and the promotion of foreign language learning. The third basket, as it stands in the Final Act, offers us little indication that the CSCE would eventually take on a new human dimension as it was first discussed at the 1989 First Meeting on the Human Dimension of the CSCE in Paris. Like the Final Act as whole, Basket III is a product of its time. In other words, the Final Act is a product of the Cold War and of Détente. Many of the issues addressed in the three baskets are largely taken for granted now, but we should not forget their importance at the time in which they were written.

The Final Act and Détente

Reflecting soon after the CSCE Helsinki negotiations, Russell states that "many delegates felt that the most significant aspect of the CSCE was that it gave substance and definition to [Détente], in that the Final Act can be viewed as a comprehensive statement of the principal elements of Détente."[42] And as we look back to the CSCE negotiations beginning in 1973, we can see that Final Act represented a particular period of time within the Cold War. As we saw in the last chapter, Détente was a result of the step back from nuclear holocaust following the Cuban Missile Crisis, the intransigence of the war in Vietnam for the Americans, and West Germany's acceptance of East Germany through Brandt's *Ostpolitik*.[43] The Final Act became the cap stone of Détente.[44] Although it was not the only thing to come out of a change in the Cold War environment, the Final Act formalized increased security and cooperation in the Euro-Atlantic area. The Final Act was meant "to broaden, deepen and make continuing and lasting the process of Détente."[45]

Nevertheless, Détente did not last, unlike the CSCE. The Soviet invasion of Afghanistan completed the general withdrawal from the spirit of Détente in both East and West, although Sivonen argues that the CSCE allowed Détente to go on much longer.[46] A meeting of the (at the time) 35 participating states of the CSCE took place in

Belgrade in 1977 to ascertain to what degree states had complied with the Final Act.[47] As was to be expected, a consensus could not be established to make a decision, which in itself says something about the nature of politics in the Euro-Atlantic area. The same happened in Madrid in 1980.[48] Although Détente did not last, the Final Act has had a lasting impact on politics in Central and Eastern Europe. For Dante B. Fascell, the Final Act is a landmark from the beginning because it allowed Western non-governmental organizations to have an unprecedented impact on international relations.[49] In an earlier work, Fascell illustrates how the Final Act was an impetus for human rights movements in Central and Eastern Europe and the Soviet Union.[50] For instance, he states:

> Soviet dissenters of varying backgrounds used the Final Act as a shelter against repression. Jews, Germans, Crimean Tatars, Baptists, Lithuanian Catholics, Russian Orthodox Christians, and nationalists from the Caucasus, the Baltic states, and Ukraine all began to cite the clauses of Principle VII (on human rights) and Basket III (on freer flow of people and information) of the [Final Act] as the basis for demanding internal change in the Soviet Union.[51]

While there had been reformist and nationalist movements in the Socialist bloc throughout the Cold War period, the Final Act gave dissident groups the moral justification for change. We can see this in the use of "Helsinki" in many of the group names, such as "Helsinki 86" in Soviet Latvia or even in the West with the "British Helsinki Human Rights Group."

Conclusion

In conclusion, the CSCE Helsinki Final Act, although without teeth as an international agreement, did give the impetus for change in the Euro-Atlantic area. Arguably, the Final Act had an impact on the timing of the end of the Cold War. Born of Détente, the Final Act laid the basis for what would become the Organization for Security and Co-operation in Europe. This chapter has offered a discussion of the Final Act and its contribution to peace and cooperation in the Cold War. The chapter also established the basis for the forthcoming transition from "conference to organization" following the end of the Cold War. This transition will be fully explored in the next chapter. We will see that Europe was "primed for peace" at the end of the Cold War.[52] The CSCE Helsinki Final Act laid the groundwork for transition.

3 From "Conference" to "Organization"

While the Helsinki Final Act set the Euro-Atlantic area on a new path to cooperation, idealism over the usual *realpolitik* of the Cold War was short-lived. The Soviet invasion of Afghanistan marked a final withdrawal from this path. Likewise, the US support for anti-communist forces around the world, for example, the Contras in Nicaragua, did little to help. While neither Afghanistan nor Nicaragua was part of the CSCE area, Soviet and American actions did little to improve trust between the two superpowers. However, the environment began to change with the dock workers strike in Poland in 1981, the change in Soviet leadership, and finally the rise to power in 1985 of Mikhail Gorbachev as Premier of the Supreme Soviet. Despite the Soviet invasions in Hungary in 1956 and Czechoslovakia in 1968, the Soviet leadership failed to send troops during the Solidarity movement in Poland in 1981. The failure to send troops to Poland to help suppress the dock workers strike illustrates a change in the Brezhnev Doctrine of military intervention in Central Europe. This showed a clear break with the Brezhnev Doctrine introduced in Chapter 2. Yet, this change could have been forecast from the signing of the Final Act. Indeed, the document says that

> [states] will respect each other's sovereign equality and individuality as well as all the rights inherent in and encompassed by its sovereignty, including in particular the right of every State to juridical equality, to territorial integrity and to freedom and political independence.

The Soviet Union had thus committed itself, although loosely, to non-interference in the CSCE area.

Leonid Brezhnev remained in power in the Soviet Union from Nikita Khrushchev's removal from power in 1964 until his death in

1982. Brezhnev's time in power is commonly referred to as a time of conservatism and stagnation within the Soviet Union.[1] With his death and subsequent quick successions of Yuri Andropov (1982–84) and Konstantin Chernenko (1984–85), the Soviet political and economic system needed a major overhaul. Following Chernenko, Gorbachev was chosen as Soviet Premier and subsequently began extensive reforms known as *glasnost* and *perestroika* to reinvigorate the political and economic stagnation. These reforms would eventually lead to the very undoing of the Soviet Union and add 15 new members to the CSCE. Most importantly, the change in the Soviet regime led to the reunification of Germany and the end of the Cold War. These changes in Europe could of course be felt within the CSCE since the Conference included participating states from both East and West. Thus, it should come as little surprise that the CSCE was one of the first international institutions to begin to change to a post-Cold War order in the Euro-Atlantic area.

As early as 1989, the participating states began to re-evaluate the current state of peace and security in Europe and the CSCE's relevance to it. From 1989 to 1996, we can see the institutionalization of the aims and objectives of the CSCE into what would become the OSCE. This chapter focuses on this transition from "Conference" to "Organization." Overall, the chapter lays out the institutional framework that we rely on in the following chapters. The chapter details the Summits/Councils and the Chairman-in-Office as the drivers of the OSCE. Structurally, the chapter details two sorts of institutions in the OSCE. First, we look at operational structures and institutions such as the Secretariat, the Chairman-in-Office, and the High Commission on National Minorities. Second, we look at decision-making bodies such as the Permanent Council, Ministerial Councils, and Summits. Finally, the chapter compels us to engage with several questions: Why was the OSCE able to grow so quickly? How was the OSCE able to come to an agreement on so much, so quickly with consensus needed among 55 participating states? Finally, how has the development within the OSCE changed over time?

A new agenda

By the end of the 1980s, East–West relations had changed for the better. Three events in 1989 illustrate the changing nature of cooperation and security in Europe. First, the Warsaw Pact and NATO countries began negotiating the Conventional Armed Forces in Europe (CFE) Treaty as a further step towards removing Soviet and American forces from Europe. The CFE Treaty was aimed at providing structure to the withdrawal and parity between Warsaw Pact and NATO forces, following on from the MBFR. Like the CSCE, the purpose was to promote trust and confidence between East and West. In particular, the CFE Treaty offered a way in which to reduce forces used in surprise attacks and large-scale invasions. While the CFE Treaty does not come under the OSCE, it does have a strong relationship with the Organization based on the Treaty's similar aims in security and cooperation. The amended CFE Treaty, for what it is worth, has even more overlap with OSCE goals, including the withdrawal of Russian forces in several frozen conflicts. While the CFE Treaty only included those member-states of the Warsaw Pact and NATO (all CSCE participating states), the negotiations illustrate how the East and West orchestrated the end of the Cold War in Europe. The nature of security in Europe had changed.

Second, in 1989, the First Meeting on the Human Dimension of the CSCE took place in Paris and was followed up again the next year in Copenhagen. Bear in mind that Basket III of the Final Act addresses the human dimension, illustrating the OSCE's commitment to "common and comprehensive" security. The final Copenhagen document set out the human dimension agenda for post-Cold War Europe: "pluralistic democracy and the rule of law are essential for ensuring respect for all human rights and fundamental freedoms." The role of the CSCE following the collapse of the Berlin Wall was to help transitioning states remain on the path to democracy and market reforms. Here, we see the first accounts of an implicit link between democracy and stability. Various democratic peace theorists have argued that democratic states are: (1) unlikely to go to war with other democratic states; (2) unlikely to go to war themselves; and (3) have limited conflicts when they do go to war.[2] While a great deal of empirical analysis has shown the democratic states are highly unlikely to go to war with other democratic states, there still remains a debate about whether democratizing states (those still in transition) are unlikely to go to war.[3] Yet, there was also an agreement that democracy was worthwhile in its own right. The democratization agenda of the CSCE was directed at "locking in" institutions and actors that would further transition.[4] The CSCE was attempting to avoid what we have seen in much of the former Soviet Union: the problem of stalled or reversed democratic transitions.[5]

The focus on the human dimension also focused on the importance of potential ethnic conflicts in the former Socialist bloc. Ethnonationalism was to lead to the dissolution of three states: the Soviet Union, Yugoslavia, and Czechoslovakia. This moment of flux was an uncomfortable period for Western Europe. On one hand, ethno-nationalism had helped bring socialist authoritarianism to an end. On the other hand, ethno-nationalism proved that it had the ability to shift borders, sometimes peacefully and at other times violently. While events in the Soviet Union and Yugoslavia had yet to come to a head, the potential for insecurity was recognized at the early stages. With this in mind, we see the CSCE participating states address "national minorities" in Paris and in Copenhagen 1990. As Rogers Brubaker has illustrated, nationalizing majorities have a tendency to rub against nationalizing minorities, which is made all the more dangerous when a minority has an external national homeland.[6] Thus, very soon following the end of the Cold War, we see the CSCE, as well as other European organizations, evolving to preserve the status quo, or in other words attempt to maintain current nation-state boundaries. This status-quo agenda remains to this day, with some notable exceptions such as the ongoing negotiations over Kosovo and the recently independent Montenegro.[7]

Finally, participating states came together in the Meeting of the Protection of the Environment in Sofia in 1989. Like ethno-nationalism, environmentalism had been a key issue that mobilized people against the socialist system. Furthermore, environmentalism was likewise a transnational issue that had the potential to affect the broader region. As Jane Dawson illustrates, in some cases environmentalism was an important part of ethno-nationalist movements in the Soviet Union.[8] For example, the Baltic republics were keenly aware of the environmental problems of the Soviet system.[9] In 1989, the meeting was aimed at countering three forms of environmental crises: industrial accidents, mismanagement of chemicals, and threats to water sources. The meeting report calls for greater coordination between participating states in order to prevent cross-border contamination. While the meeting illustrates the environment's importance to the CSCE agenda in the early post-Cold War period, it has not remained thus. In fact, while the CSCE/OSCE has developed a great number of institutions to cope with different forms of security and democracy, there are none specifically focused on the environment despite it falling within Basket II of the Final Act. Recently, however, some participating states have attempted to put the environment and the economy back onto the OSCE agenda.

Thus, the CSCE saw itself facing three key challenges: state collapse, stalled transitions, and transnational crises. The end of the Cold War was precipitated by an initial liberalization. In some states, such as Poland, Hungary, and the Czech Republic, liberalization led to democratic transition and eventually liberal democracy. However, the majority of states in the former Socialist bloc did not progress from liberalization, to democratization, to liberal democracy, but rather something in-between. States in Central and Eastern Europe faced a series of challenges from stalled political and economic reform, corruption, or the outbreak of violence.[10] The OSCE has been primarily engaged with those states that, for one reason or another, have stalled in their efforts to democratize.

To some degree, despite the early response by the CSCE, crises have happened in these three areas. As mentioned, the Euro-Atlantic area saw the collapse of three multi-ethnic states where only Czechoslovakia "divorced" peacefully. We are still living with the ramifications of conflict in the former Soviet Union and Yugoslavia. Second, while the majority of participating states have either consolidated their transitions to democracy or are on the road to democratization following armed conflict, some have either stalled or faltered altogether. Belarus remains an authoritarian state despite the willingness to dress it up as "democratic," while Central Asian states range from the slow liberalizing steps of Kyrgyzstan to the neo-sultanate of Turkmenistan. Nevertheless, all the participating states in Central and Eastern Europe are fully committed to democracy. The OSCE has had a part to play in the democratic states, the democratizing states, and the faltering states throughout the Euro-Atlantic region. Finally, environmental degradation remains a problem particularly in those areas that are poorest. For example, the status of the Caspian Sea remains unstable particularly because of its multi-national location. While much of the region has been unstable since the end of the Cold War, the CSCE has helped mitigate these crises while preventing others. The Conference did this by establishing institutions with which to cope with the new challenges of the post-Cold War era. In this regard, the "Conference on" became the "Organization for."

Institution-building in the OSCE

The transition from "Conference" to "Organization" can be dated to the adoption of the Charter of Paris for a New Europe by participating states in November 1990. The Charter of Paris established a permanent Secretariat, the Conflict Prevention Centre in Vienna, and the Office for Free Elections (the forerunner of ODIHR) in Warsaw. Two things are clear when we consider the locations of the first CSCE institutions. First, while the EU, NATO, and the Council of Europe are based in Western Europe (Belgium and France), the CSCE Secretariat, and Office for Free Elections were based in cities in

Central Europe. These locations illustrate the CSCE's early intentions of focusing primarily on the regions "East of Vienna." Second, the OSCE is different in that it has placed its institutions across Europe. Currently, there are OSCE institutions in Vienna, Warsaw, The Hague, and Copenhagen. The decision to have a decentralized organization was a strategy to prevent the development of a large, centralized bureaucracy.[11] In addition to a skeletal bureaucracy on the ground, the Charter of Paris also set limits on staffing arrangements, limiting individuals to two years with a possible extension of one year. Overall, the organization has less than 450 members of staff working within OSCE institutions, as well as over 3,000 in field operations. The 2006 budget, as dictated by the Permanent Council, was 168,165,800 euros. While this has meant that the OSCE's "centripetal" and "centrifugal" forces remain restrained, it also impairs the organization's ability to operate, especially in terms of losing institutional knowledge.

The Charter of Paris established a system of secondment for staff recruitment. Basically, this means that a participating state submits an individual for an OSCE position which is then confirmed by the Ministerial Council, an annual meeting of foreign ministers. Accordingly, a participating state is only allowed to occupy one seconded position in the OSCE institutions, unless no other state is willing to second its national for the vacant position. The cost of a seconded post is paid for by the participating state, rather than the OSCE core budget. The OSCE also has contracted positions where particular expertise is needed or for administrative and clerical posts. As we will see later, there has been criticism of the OSCE bureaucracy as of late and there are reform proposals to make positions more "professional."

In 1992, the CSCE established two new institutions to deal with threats to stability and security in the *Helsinki Document: the Challenges of Change*. The Forum for Security and Cooperation (FSC) was established in response to several events. First, prior to the Helsinki Document, the CSCE had agreed on the *Vienna Document on Confidence- and Security-Building Measures* in March which established a system of exchanging information on strategic resources, such as troops, equipment, and budgets. Second, and also in March, the *Treaty on Open Skies* established a regime for observation flights. While not an OSCE agreement, it fits well within the remit of the organization's aims of security and cooperation. However, there was a subsequent CSCE Declaration on the Treaty on Open Skies which "[assessed] the Treaty as an important element in the process of enhancing security." Lastly, the CFE Treaty agreed in 1989 finally came into force shortly after the Helsinki Document. Like the Vienna

Document and the Open Skies Treaty, the CFE Treaty established a regime of confidence-building and political trust. Incidentally, the administrations of the Open Skies and CFE Treaties are located in Vienna and, like the UK, many participating states deal with them from within their delegations to the OSCE.

The Helsinki Document also created the position of a High Commissioner on National Minorities. Mirroring the change in terminology from "Conference" to "Organization," the position was created high commissioner "on" rather than "for" minorities. Conflict in the former Soviet Union and Yugoslavia between ethnic majorities and minorities as well as perceived discrimination against Russians in the Baltic States, Hungarians in Slovakia and Romania, and Turks in Bulgaria (to name only a few), illustrated a need to confront potential ethnic conflicts before they occurred. Jennifer Jackson Preece has defined "national minorities" as

> a group numerically inferior to the rest of the population of a state, in a non-dominant position, well-defined, and historically established on the territory of the state, whose members – being nationals of the state – possess ethnic, religious, linguistic or cultural characteristics differing from those of the rest of the population and show, if only implicitly, a sense of solidarity, directed towards preserving their culture, traditions, religion, or language.[12]

The focus on "national" minorities is interesting because it precludes the inclusion of immigrants or refugees. Again, the High Commissioner's remit is an indication of where the CSCE perceived its work to be: in the East. The problems of national minorities in Central and Eastern Europe had been long, troublesome and the catalyst to at least one world war. With the Helsinki Document, the CSCE established the only institution among international organizations to deal specifically with national minorities.

On 6 December 1994, a summit of Heads of State from participating states in Budapest agreed to change the "Conference" to the "Organization."[13] The Budapest Summit Declaration states, "we are determined to give a new political impetus to the CSCE, thus enabling it to play a cardinal role in meeting the challenges of the twenty-first century. To reflect this determination, the CSCE will henceforth be known as the [OSCE]." By the time of the change in name, the great bulk of the organization had already been established. Only the OSCE Representative on Freedom of the Media would be established afterwards in 1997. Overall, the structure of OSCE is unlike any other international organization. In particular, other than the Heads of State summits and annual Ministerial Councils, there is no discernible hierarchy. Many of the institutions such as ODIHR and the High Commissioner are autonomous entities within the OSCE; again, another issue that some participating states would like to see addressed. Nevertheless, agenda-setting primarily lies with the rotating Chairman-in-Office, the OSCE Troika leadership, and the Summits/Ministerial Councils. Let us take a look at each in turn, beginning with the operational structures and institutions.

OSCE operational structures and institutions

The OSCE Secretariat

The OSCE Secretariat, located in Vienna, forms the bureaucracy of the organization. As we will see in many cases in this chapter, a great deal has been written about the OSCE missions and the High Commissioner, but very little has been written in regards to many of the OSCE institutions. The Secretariat is our first example. The Secretariat is directed by the Secretary General, who holds the post for three years. The Secretary General acts as the chief administrative officer in the OSCE. Since June 2005, the current Secretary General has been Ambassador Marc Perrin de Brichambaut, from France. Thus far, the four Secretaries General have come from diplomatic service backgrounds. The Secretary General works as a representative of the current Chairman-in-Office (CiO). The rotational system means that a Secretary General will work with three CiOs during their term.

As we can see from Figure 3.1, the Secretariat has many issue areas in its remit. The issue-specific sections in the Secretariat have grown with time and have largely been dictated by the Ministerial Councils and CiOs. The oldest is the Conflict Prevention Centre (CPC) created by the Charter of Paris in 1990. The CPC addresses the security aims of the Final Act's first basket. When created, the CPC's main aim was to support confidence- and security-building measures (or CSBMs). At the third Ministerial Council in Stockholm in 1992, the participating states requested that the CPC organize information exchanges in the field regarding early warning and peacekeeping techniques. The Stockholm Council allowed the CPC to have a presence in the field by establishing and supporting the organization's field missions and other field activities, including supplying personnel, logistics, and training. The CPC's development has been greatly influenced by events in the former Yugoslavia, where the OSCE established a mission to FYR Macedonia in 1992, Bosnia-Herzegovina in 1995 and a verification mission in Kosovo in 1998. The Charter for European Security agreed by the participating states at the 1999 Istanbul Summit added the Operation Planning Centre to CPC, established to facilitate OSCE missions and field activities. The Charter also limited the mandate of the CPC by creating a new recruitment unit known as the Rapid Expert Assistance and Cooperation Teams (REACT), who supply personnel for missions and field activities. As we discuss in Chapters 4 and 5, missions remain one of the most advantageous features of the OSCE and thus the CPC remains a vital part of the OSCE.

The Secretariat contains several units that deal with transnational issues. First, in response to the events of 11 September 2001, the OSCE responded by adding an Action against Terrorism Unit to the Secretariat. The mandate was given by the Bucharest Plan of Action for Combating Terrorism, created in December 2001. The main objective of the Anti-Terrorism Unit is capacity-building among participating states to deal with the threat of terrorism. Second, the Maastricht Ministerial Council in 2003 created the Special Representative on Combating Trafficking in Human Beings. Like the Anti-Terrorism Unit, the job of the Special Representative is capacity-building across participating states. In addition, the Anti-Trafficking Unit is also responsible for liaising with other international organizations in regards to human trafficking, such as the Council of Europe. Otherwise, like all the units in the Secretariat, the Anti-Trafficking Unit is able to offer expert, technical advice on fighting trafficking in human beings. Third, the Office of the Coordinator of OSCE Economic and Environmental Activities, also created by the Maastricht Ministerial Council, has a mandate that combines Baskets I and II of the Final Act. Specifically, the Economic and Environmental Activities Unit is a resource for economic, social, and environmental aspects of security across the organization. The nature of international organization is to deal with issue areas that ordinarily fall outside the remit of individual nation-states. These three Secretariat units bring us back to the Charter of Paris and the challenges of post-Cold War Europe. With these units, the Secretariat provides a technical base to deal with the transnational challenges of the Euro-Atlantic area. However, considering the early focus on transnational threats to security, seen also in the Charter of Paris, it is incongruous that it took the organization until after 2001 to develop such issue-specific resources.

Two additional units in the Secretariat are worth mentioning here. Following the conflicts in the former Yugoslavia and the OSCE field activities, the OSCE developed a unit for orchestrating police training.

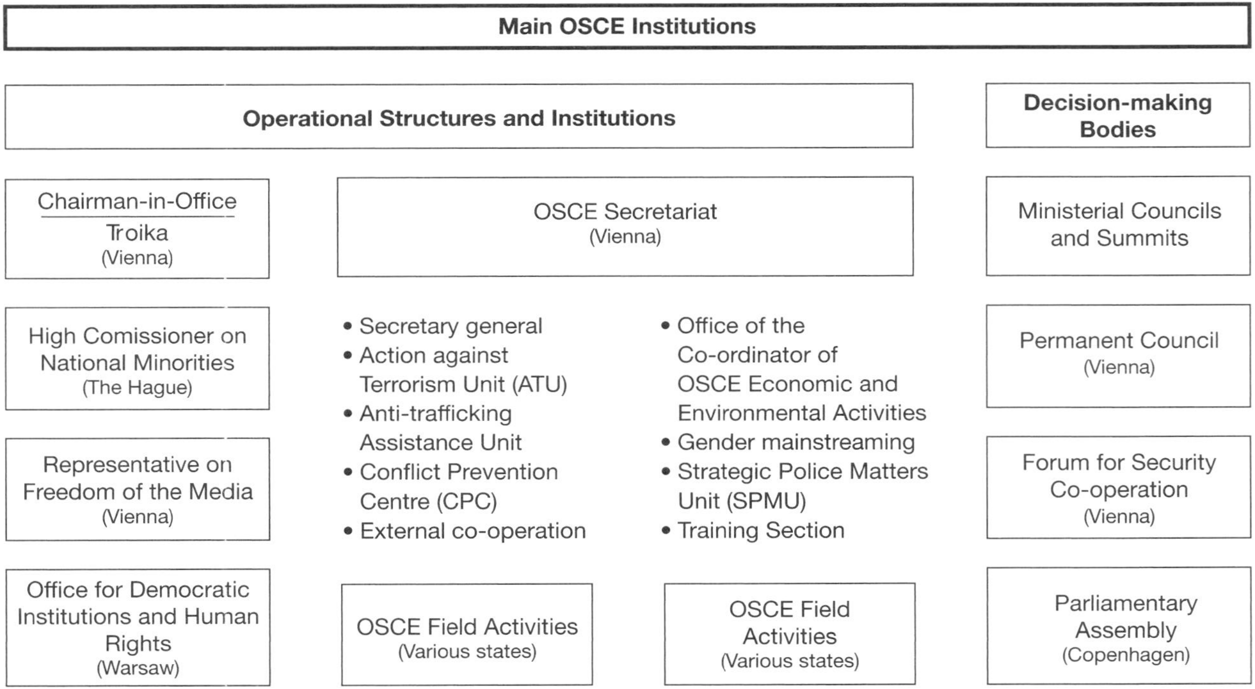

Main OSCE Institutions

Operational Structures and Institutions		Decision-making Bodies

Chairman-in-Office Troika (Vienna)

High Comissioner on National Minorities (The Hague)

Representative on Freedom of the Media (Vienna)

Office for Democratic Institutions and Human Rights (Warsaw)

OSCE Secretariat (Vienna)

- Secretary general
- Action against Terrorism Unit (ATU)
- Anti-trafficking Assistance Unit
- Conflict Prevention Centre (CPC)
- External co-operation

- Office of the Co-ordinator of OSCE Economic and Environmental Activities
- Gender mainstreaming
- Strategic Police Matters Unit (SPMU)
- Training Section

OSCE Field Activities (Various states)

OSCE Field Activities (Various states)

Ministerial Councils and Summits

Permanent Council (Vienna)

Forum for Security Co-operation (Vienna)

Parliamentary Assembly (Copenhagen)

Figure 3.1 Main OSCE institutions.

In 2001, the Strategic Police Matters Unit was established. The Policing Unit has a network of advisors as part of OSCE missions in FYR Macedonia, Kosovo, Croatia, Serbia and Montenegro, and Kyrgyzstan. Finally, the Section for External Cooperation orchestrates the OSCE's collaboration, coordination, and information exchanges between it and other international organizations and actors. While the OSCE (and the CSCE before it) has always attempted to cooperate with other actors, it was not until the Charter of European Security (1999) that a clear mandate was established. The Permanent Council created the Section for External Cooperation the following year.[14] This section represents the future of the OSCE, where the need for cooperation, coordination, and burden-sharing has become more important since EU and NATO enlargement. As we shall see, other regional and international organizations are never very far away when it comes to OSCE activities and thus it is only fitting that the Secretariat has the ability to orchestrate these liaisons.

The Chairman-in-Office and the Troika system[15]

The Charter for Paris (1990) called for a chairman to direct the "Committee of Senior Officials" (later to become the Permanent Council), which would basically carry out the business of the Ministerial Councils. The Chairman-in-Office (CiO) is derived from this statement in the Charter of Paris. However, the CiO as an institution unto itself was established in the Helsinki Council Decisions (1992). Thus, this explains why the first "chairman" (Hans-Dietrich Genscher of Germany) was in fact instated a year before the CiO position had been created in name. The foreign minister of the participating state for that year takes on the role of the CiO. The CiO is the most prominent representative of the OSCE. She or he is responsible for maintaining information exchanges among different institutions in the OSCE. The CiO will also dictate an agenda for the OSCE while that participating state holds the CiO position. For instance, the CiO for 2006 was held by Belgian Foreign Minister Karel De Gucht. Belgium's aims have been:

- promoting the rule of law;
- fighting against organized crime;
- balancing the three dimensions;
- institutional reform;
- progress on "frozen conflict";
- maintaining an important role for OSCE in Kosovo.[16]

Several participating states have used the CiO position to great effect, such as the Netherlands in 2003 and Bulgaria in 2004. The CiO is the key agenda-setter within the OSCE. Although no state has been CiO more than once, there is no rotational system to allocate positions. Thus far, there has been a preponderance of participating states from Western, Central, and Northern Europe.

The CiO is helped by the so-called "Troika," which consists of the preceding, present and succeeding chairmanships. Thus, in 2006 this was Slovenia, Belgium and Spain. The purpose of the Troika is to give some degree of institutional memory to a post that only lasts one year. The Troika system also means that initiatives are unlikely to be dropped as soon as a given state no longer fills the CiO. Furthermore, as the CiOs are foreign ministers, there is a great deal to do with managing the OSCE while orchestrating a state's foreign policy. Together, the CiO as part of the Troika adds political consistency and stability to the OSCE.

The High Commissioner on National Minorities (HCNM)[17]

Created in the 1992 Helsinki Document and then refined in the 1996 Lisbon Document, the High Commissioner on National Minorities (or HCNM) is arguably the most innovative institution in the OSCE.[18] As stated earlier, the HCNM is the only instrument across international organizations to deal specifically with national minorities. While there has been some discussion about establishing similar institutions in other regions and organizations, there are considerable hurdles to overcome such as nation-state fears of unwarranted interference.[19] The first High Commissioner was Max van der Stoel. The seasoned and well-respected former Dutch Foreign Minister played an important part in establishing this mechanism for dealing with national minorities. The role of the HCNM is primarily an early warning mechanism for conflict prevention where national minorities are involved. Of the post-Cold War conflicts in the former Socialist bloc, all have an element of ethnic conflict. The High Commissioner is predicated on "quiet diplomacy." The HCNM performs this role by observation, negotiation, and recommendation. Often, the High Commissioner makes field visits to areas that have perceived problematic relationships between majorities and minorities. In these visits, the High Commissioner is able to meet with all sides and to probe areas of constructive dialogue. Upon the High Commissioner's return, the HCNM issues a set of country-specific recommendations for the participating state visited. Under van der Stoel, the HCNM recommendations were often made public. However, Ambassador Rolf Ekeus has adhered strictly to "quiet diplomacy." This change in policy of the HCNM may be because the terms of negotiation have changed as the states under consideration have narrowed. Previous work by the High Commissioner with some of the 2004 EU enlargement states had a different context than that of other states. In particular, the acceding states were more sensitive to negative portrayals as they attempted to gain EU membership. The same cannot be said for Belarus or Kyrgyzstan, for instance.

The HCNM often relies on agreed norms derived from other international organizations on which to press a case. For example, the High Commissioner has often referred to UN and Council of Europe conventions on human rights in his statements. At the same time, the HCNM has been important in creating new standards for the treatment of national minorities. The HCNM has sponsored several meetings of minority rights experts from the Foundation on Inter-Ethnic Relations to formulate specific criteria. Five such documents have come out of the OSCE-sponsored meetings. The first was the 1996 Hague Recommendations Regarding the Education Rights of National Minorities. The Hague Recommendations stress the need for mutual bilingualism in society. In theory, bilingualism should encourage empathy and reciprocity which in turn would lead to confidence-building among the groups. Bilingualism would also be a safe way of precluding forced or unforced assimilation. Second, the 1998 Oslo Recommendations Regarding the Linguistic Rights of National Minorities go beyond educational needs to focus on the role of language in the public sphere. Much of what is in the Oslo Recommendations can also be found in the Council of Europe's Framework Convention for the Protection of National Minorities, including the use of minority languages in areas where that group may predominate. Third, there is the 1999 Lund Recommendations on the Effective Participation of National Minorities in Public Life, which establish expectations of minority involvement in politics and society.

Recently, Ekeus has orchestrated two additional sets of guidelines or recommendations, dealing with language use in broadcasting and inter-ethnic policing. The Guidelines on the Use of Minority Languages in the Broadcast Media were created in October 2003. The broadcasting guidelines were a result of significant interest by OSCE participating states in issues concerning media and minorities at the March 2001 OSCE Supplementary Human Dimension Meeting on Freedom of Expression. The High Commissioner also worked with the OSCE Representative on Freedom of the Media in designing the recommendations. Additionally, the High Commissioner has recently orchestrated the design of the Recommendations on Policing in Multi-Ethnic

Societies in February 2006. The Recommendations were the result of encounters while visiting the field. In some cases, participating states had little experience of either managing police–society relations or a process of building representative police forces. Like all of the recommendations (and guidelines), the policing recommendations are a mixture of legal obligations and best-practices. Taken all together, these recommendations have established specific criteria for the treatment of national minorities, an area that has customarily been dealt with in differing ways.

The Office for Democratic Institutions and Human Rights (ODIHR)

ODIHR most clearly represents OSCE's attempt to address the human dimension. The institution's objectives were expanded with the 1992 Helsinki Document to incorporate democratization, human rights, gender equality, tolerance and non-discrimination, and elections. While an autonomous institution within the OSCE, ODIHR can be requested by the CiO to take on special responsibilities. Otherwise, ODIHR is run by a director, who since March 2003 has been Ambassador Christian Strohal of Austria. Randolf Oberschmidt argues that initially while ODIHR was able to ensure democratic principles and basic human rights, it had little success in other areas.[20] In essence, this was the case because ODIHR lacked professional depth. This changed after the internal reforms in 1997, confirmed by the Copenhagen Document of the same year. The reform led to greater investment in personnel in addition to clearer objective targets and strategies. Since then, ODIHR has gone further beyond simply monitoring and information exchange to offering technical assistance. Especially under the present director, there has been a move towards a professional, expert-led ODIHR. Incidentally, ODIHR's budget is not limited to core budget allocations.[21] In fact, the institution benefits from funding from Western states that see ODIHR's work as fitting in with their own foreign policy objectives in the former Socialist bloc.

ODIHR's work in the field is primarily done through the field missions. ODIHR is usually able to operate within missions with broad mandates. Where the mandate centers on conflict prevention alone, ODIHR is less likely to have input.[22] For example, ODIHR has been accused by the Russian Federation of being behind the democratization movements in Georgia and Ukraine in 2003 and 2004 respectively. While it is unlikely that ODIHR pressed for regime change, the institution had supported non-governmental organizations (NGOs) in both states through OSCE field missions prior to the Rose and

Orange Revolutions. In this regard, despite the broad agenda of ODIHR, its election monitoring remains the most visible function. In response to the claims of participating states in the post-Soviet region that there is a regional bias in the OSCE, ODIHR began to monitor elections throughout the OSCE region beginning with the US congressional elections in 2002.

The Charter for European Security (1999) called on increased cooperation between European organizations in particular. Like several other institutions in the OSCE, ODIHR has been at the forefront of growing relationships between the OSCE and other international organizations. Considering ODIHR's remit, it is no surprise that the Council of Europe is one of its key partners.[23] In several field locations, the OSCE has a common office with the Council of Europe. This increased relationship with the Council of Europe and other bodies like the European Commission is important because of the increased overlap across especially European organizations. In particular, the work of ODIHR is addressed, to one degree or another, by both the Council of Europe and the EU. Thus, the increased professional, expert-led nature of ODIHR is an important development if the OSCE wants to continue to offer a distinct contribution to European security and cooperation.

The Representative on Freedom of the Media[24]

Along with ODIHR and the HCNM, the OSCE Representative on Freedom of the Media (FOM) is the last of the three institutions that deal with the human dimension of comprehensive security. The Lisbon Ministerial Summit (1996) called for the establishment of the FOM, which came into being in 1997. Naturally, the FOM is predicated on ensuring that participating states live up to OSCE principles and commitments in regard to freedom of expression and free media. Its primary activities are ensuring that participating states refrain from obstructing media activities, in addition to ensuring that journalists are not treated unfavorably. Like the HCNM, the FOM is an early warning mechanism for the OSCE. When the FOM does recognize an instance of non-compliance, it can deploy rapidly to engage with the state that has potentially transgressed. The FOM can report a transgressing state to the CiO and Permanent Council, where further recommendations can be made regarding appropriate action by the OSCE.

Like the other bodies in the OSCE, the FOM is primarily aimed at countries in the East. For instance, in his regular report in December 2005, the current Representative, Miklos Haraszti from Hungary, gave details of 12 participating states that had allegedly violated OSCE commitments.[25] Of the 12, only the United States and Germany were not east of Vienna. Perhaps the most significant challenge for the FOM has been the "Danish cartoons" controversy. The FOM explained to the Permanent Council why the Danish newspaper, *Jyllands-Posten*, published the cartoons and criticized the paper for not addressing the concerns of readers who would be offended by the publication.[26] The FOM also criticized the violence that came in response. The Regular Report also suggested ways in which to move on from the crisis, such as governments maintaining a distance between themselves and the publishers as well as promoting responsibility in freedom. The events surrounding the cartoons illustrate the important nature of FOM. In particular, it illustrates the insecurities that can come from irresponsible governments and the media.

While the OSCE as an organization has established a series of provisions to deal with freedom of expression, information, and media, the FOM has gone further in establishing in-depth guidelines for member-states in a similar vein to the HCNM. Thus far, the FOM has addressed three areas. First, the FOM has attempted to address the use of criminal libel and insult laws in the aptly named, *Ending the Chilling Effect*.[27] Criminal libel and insult laws are typical methods used by authoritative governments to control journalistic investigation. Second, the FOM has set out a series of standards to deal with media freedom and the internet.[28] Third and most recently, the FOM has established recommendations for editorial independence.[29] Editorial independence is essential for a free media but also allows for a self-regulating media which can produce a healthy relationship between politics, society, and the media itself. There are other documents produced by the FOM that deal specifically with certain regions (e.g. Central Asia) where freedom of the media remains most at risk. Across different regions, the FOM faces different problems, such as post-Soviet legacies, balancing freedom and security, and simply general inexperience with a free media. Nevertheless, the most recent institution in the OSCE has done its part in establishing standards with which to make recommendations. Policy-making becomes policy implementation when institutions such as the FOM work through the missions and field activities.

Missions and other field activities

As we have seen thus far, many of the institutions within the OSCE use the missions and other field activities as a way of addressing many of the issues surrounding security and cooperation in the region. Missions come in many different sizes, mandates, durations and, interestingly, titles. Ordinarily, size and mandate are strongly correlated. Thus, a single issue mandate may, but does not necessarily, require a smaller field presence. Furthermore, mandate can be strongly related to duration. For instance, addressing a single-issue area may, but not necessarily, take less time than a mandate that has several issue areas. Finally, largely for political reasons, the missions have been given a variety of titles, the best-known being the former "OSCE Assistance Group to Chechnya." The OSCE's missions and other field activities are managed by the CPC in the OSCE Secretariat as established by the Stockholm Council in 1992.

As Box 3.1 illustrates, the OSCE's missions and other field activities cover a large geographical area.[30] The OSCE's field activities are customarily based on a consensus decision by the Permanent Council and the acceptance of the participating state involved. The OSCE long-term missions generally have a limited mandate. For instance, the first long-term mission to be established was the OSCE Spillover Monitor Mission to Skopje in 1992, which is still ongoing at the time of writing. The mission to Skopje was, in fact, an extension of the European Community Monitoring Mission to neighboring countries of the Federal Yugoslav Republic.[31] The mandate, as set out by the CSO (the forerunner of the Permanent Council) was to monitor the border between FYR Macedonia and Yugoslavia. The mandate also set out to ensure territorial integrity of both states. To offer an example of numbers, the OSCE Spillover Monitor Mission to Skopje has 104 international personnel, but this is only an end result of a fluctuation from a minimum of four personnel to a total of 210 in September 2001.[32] Not all missions last this long. In fact, as Box 3.1 illustrates, the OSCE has closed eight missions as of 2006. In some cases, such as Estonia and Latvia, the missions were seen to have been successful and were closed in December 2001.[33] Others, like the OSCE Assistance Group to Chechnya, became untenable due to a serious deterioration of security. The mandate was not extended and thus it closed in March 2003.[34]

The OSCE field offices and centers ordinarily have a much broader mandate. All the field offices and centers were established after 1997, although the OSCE Centre in Dushanbe was formerly referred to as the OSCE Mission to Tajikistan (established in 1993) and the OSCE Centre in Tashkent was formerly known as the OSCE Liaison Office in Central Asia (established in 1995). The offices and centers are a route for OSCE activities in general. In general, their mandates are aimed at

Box 3.1 OSCE field missions and other field activities

OSCE missions

- Bosnia and Herzegovina
- Croatia
- Georgia
- Kosovo
- Moldova
- Serbia*
- Montenegro*
- OSCE Spillover Monitor Mission to Skopje

OSCE centers

- Almaty
- Ashgabad
- Bishkek
- Dushanbe
- Tashkent
- OSCE Presence in Albania
- OSCE Project Co-ordinator in Ukraine
- The Personal Representative of the CiO on the Conflict Dealt with by the OSCE Minsk Conference

OSCE offices

- Baku
- Minsk
- Yerevan

Closed field activities

- OSCE Mission of Long Duration in Kosovo, Sandjak, Vojvodina
- OSCE Kosovo Verification Mission
- OSCE Representative to the Joint Committee on the Skrunda Radar Station
- OSCE Mission to Ukraine
- OSCE Mission to Estonia
- OSCE Mission to Latvia

- OSCE Assistance Group to Chechnya
- OSCE Advisory and Monitoring Group in Belarus

Source: *Fact Sheet: What Is the OSCE?* www.osce.org/secretariat/item_11_13554.html (accessed: 19 June 2006) and (OSCE Secretariat 2005).

Notes:
* The OSCE Mission to Serbia and Montenegro was changed to the OSCE Mission to Serbia and a new OSCE Mission to Montenegro was established on 29 June 2006 by the OSCE Permanent Council.

facilitating cooperation between OSCE institutions, the CiO and the participating state. As an indication of the broad tasks an office or center may have, the OSCE Project Coordinator in Ukraine states:

> This co-operation will be based on the planning, implementation and monitoring of projects between relevant authorities of Ukraine and the OSCE and its institutions. *Such projects may cover all aspects of OSCE activities* and may involve governmental as well as non-governmental bodies of Ukraine.[35]

Furthermore, autonomous institutions such as ODIHR may use the facilities to launch projects in the participating states. An example is the HCNM's focus on policing in inter-ethnic communities in Kyrgyzstan.[36] As we will see in the next chapters, the field activities are one of the OSCE's main assets. Furthermore, as we will discuss in the final chapter, the field activities offer the OSCE a tool and skill-set that other regional organizations do not have. When considering the future of the OSCE, we must keep the field activities in mind.

The Parliamentary Assembly

The parliamentary dimension of the OSCE sits in Copenhagen, established by the Charter of Paris (1990) to facilitate cooperation between national legislatures. Parliamentarians are elected by their respective national assemblies and meet in the winter and spring sessions, each year. The purpose of the OSCE Parliamentary Assembly's (PA) creation is four-fold. First, a parliamentary assembly was seen as being helpful in the socialization of democratic transition. Parliamentarians would be acquainted with democratic rules and procedures that they could then employ/maintain at home. Furthermore, parliamentarians from "transitioning" states could "rub elbows" with parliamentarians from "consolidated states," allowing for collegial socialization. Second, the PA promotes greater involvement in the OSCE by national parliaments. Such a liaison between the OSCE and leading politicians is a way to maintain interest in the organization. Third, the OSCE PA has become a key part of the election-monitoring regime. The PA uses parliamentarians as election experts in the OSCE region. For a relevant election in the OSCE area, the CiO appoints a senior parliamentarian in the PA to act as a special coordinator to oversee short-term monitoring missions. These PA missions run parallel to those of ODIHR, similar to those of the European Parliament or PACE. While it would seem less than ideal to have a parliamentarian from a less than democratic participating state observing elections, in practice PA coordinators have often been critical of such states attempting to "undermine" the election monitoring process.[37] Finally, the PA is able to make recommendations through declarations concerning the whole of the OSCE. Most recently, the PA has been a source of reform recommendations, which we will discuss in the final chapter.

OSCE decision-making bodies

Ministerial Councils and summits

The transition from "Conference" to "Organization" is a direct result of the ministerial councils and summits. In essence, the CSCE was a series of councils and summits before the organization became institutionalized in 1990. The Ministerial Councils are annual except in years when there is a summit. The first ministerial meeting took place in Helsinki on 3–7 July 1973, referred to then as the CSCE Ministers of Foreign Affairs. The Councils are where participating state foreign ministers meet to discuss the organization. Summits, on the other hand, are periodic where heads of state or government meet. The first summit took place in Helsinki from 30 July–1 August 1975 and the most recent at the time of writing has been the Istanbul Summit in 1999. Councils and summits are held by the participating state that currently holds the CiO. For example, the 2005 Ministerial Council was held in Slovenia. We can see that in the creation of the institutions discussed in this chapter, they have all been created as a result of the conclusions of a council or summit. Remarkably, the councils and summits have been able to come to agreed conclusions over the years despite consensus voting. The OSCE has ceased to "deepen" further currently, with the last major innovation being the establishment of the FOM. Council and summit conclusions are more likely to be issue-oriented rather than aimed at institution building within the organization. This change is partly to do with a change in politics between participating states, as we will discuss further.

The Permanent Council and delegations to the OSCE

The Council of Senior Officials (or "CSO Vienna Group") created in the Charter of Paris (1990) was the beginning of the transition from "Conference" to "Organization." The FSO became the Permanent Council (PC) following the Stockholm Council in 1992. The PC is akin to a legislature in a governmental structure or similar to the United Nations General Assembly.[38] At the same time, the PC has more agenda-setting power than does the European Parliament. In essence, the PC is where the participating state delegations to the OSCE sit around a table to discuss a set agenda. The agenda is first set out by the CiO but is then added to by other delegations. Ordinarily, the PC meets in the stately Hofburg in Vienna every Thursday. Ambassadors or their deputies sit around the table in French alphabetical order. The PC can meet in emergency sessions if required and can also establish sub-committees, for example, on the human dimension. Other than the annual Councils or Summits, the PC is the main agenda-setting body in the OSCE. For instance, the PC is the institution that created the many missions and field activities discussed previously. Furthermore, the PC is a customary outlet for the objectives of the CiO. Decisions, when they are taken, are based on consensus voting. It is routine that motions do not make it to the floor unless consensus is expected.

Consensus means that participating state delegations must work together to achieve decision-making. Delegations, like the state that they represent, are of varying sizes. Size is partly based on state size and international influence. For example, the Americans and Russians have quite large delegations. On the other hand, a delegation's size is also based on how much the participating state believes the OSCE is important. Furthermore, the member-states of the EU tend to work together, allowing the country holding the European Council Presidency to speak for the 25 member-states in the PC when agreement can be achieved. Thus, EU member-states do not need to keep as large a delegation as perhaps they once had. Delegations often cooperate as we would expect. Friends or allies in other international arenas overlap with cooperation in the OSCE. At the same time, informal delegation traits may play an important role, such as regarding which languages personnel speak or those who socialize more readily. In such cases of informal cooperation, formal negotiations are easier.[39]

Delegations to the OSCE are ordinarily a part of the participating states' foreign ministries. Political culture and domestic context will dictate to what degree a delegation has autonomy *vis-à-vis* its capital. As politicians have to play their own two-level games domestically and abroad when making foreign policy, so delegations often have to coordinate and in some cases converge the interests of the state and the OSCE.[40] Arguably, the most difficult position for a delegation is not when the capital is demanding something different from the majority of other states, but rather when ambassadors and their delegations are unsure about what their governments want. The last thing an ambassador wants is a rebuke from her/his capital. Nevertheless, this is the nature of international diplomacy and participation in international organizations can highlight information costs. The PC and its delegation representations make many of the essential decisions for the OSCE. Where the OSCE Secretariat is the "nuts and bolts" of the OSCE machine, the PC is headed by the CiO is ordinarily its "driver."

The Forum for Security Cooperation (FSC)[41]

At the end of the Cold War, many states in Central and Eastern Europe had large, out-of-date arsenals predicated on fighting a Western invasion.[42] The FSC was established by the Helsinki Document (1992) to deal with the problems of the post-Cold War era specifically in terms of politico-military security. This dimension deals with democratic control of all security forces, international humanitarian law and principles governing the use of force. The FSC meets weekly in Vienna. The current activities of the FSC take several forms. First, the FSC provides assistance with small arms based on the OSCE Document on Small Arms and Light Weapons (2000).[43] The countries of the former Socialist bloc are fertile sources of legal and illegal small arms. Not only has this inflamed conflict in the OSCE region, but also in other areas of the world. Second, the FSC provides assistance with ammunition based on the OSCE Document on Stockpiles of Conventional Ammunition (2003).[44] The focus in this case is on surplus stockpiles of ammunition that can pose security risks both in forms of conflict and environmental degradation. Third, the FSC provides assistance projects specifically in Belarus and Tajikistan, who have both requested assistance in destroying surplus arms. The FSC decisions within the Lisbon Document (1996) allowed the establishment of assistance projects when requested by participating states. Finally, and most importantly, the FSC facilitates information exchange as part of its overall goal of confidence- and security-building measures. This information exchange overlaps with related non-OSCE bodies such as the Joint Consultative Group for the CFE Treaty and the Open Skies Commission. Although part of the transition from "Conference" to "Organization," the FSC goes back to the heart of the inter-governmental nature of the CSCE.

The Economic Forum

Lest we forget that the end of the Cold War brought about a dual transition for countries in the former Socialist bloc (political and economic), the OSCE Economic Forum was established in 1992 by the Helsinki Document. The Economic Forum was established to allow the Permanent Council to reconvene to discuss the second dimension specifically. The Economic Forum meets once a year to discuss economic and environmental aspects of security. The prime objectives are fighting against corruption, organized crime, and environmental degradation. Similar to the FSC, the Economic Forum has become a focal point for expert knowledge on such issues. In this regard, the Economic Forum orchestrates regional workshops on economic and environmental challenges to security. Nevertheless, the Economic Forum's status in the OSCE is not that of FSC. If we look back at the institutions discussed, we can see that the focus in the OSCE has been and is primarily on the first (politico-military) and third (human) dimensions of security. The second dimension has largely been relegated by the OSCE, a point that some participating states (the Russian Federation and co.) are looking to rectify in reforms of the organization. At the same time, other states (the United States and co.) are unwilling to move the focus onto the second dimension if it is to the detriment of the third dimension. This situation illustrates the stasis currently in the OSCE. Remarkably, the consensus on the transition from "Conference" to "Organization" was much greater. How did this consensus happen?

The politics of "deepening"

Evolution in the process of European integration has often been referred to as "widening" and "deepening."[45] Widening, in the case of the OSCE, has been the result of three failed states that we mentioned earlier. Deepening, on the other hand, has been the subject of this chapter. The participating states of the CSCE were aware of the challenges to security and cooperation in the region. The *Zeitgeist* following the end of the Cold War also encouraged multi-lateral mechanisms to engage with these challenges. The interests of the "West" can be easily seen in the CSCE's transition to the OSCE. North America and Western Europe were keen to see stability in the East. Security meant democracy, and democracy meant capitalism. All three favored the West. The CSCE was the only organization that was able to encompass comprehensive security and also included the nation-states of both East and West. Naturally, the CSCE was the organization to do this. The interests of the Eastern governments were mixed. The majority of the Central and Eastern European governments were keen to "lock-in" democratic institutions and continue market reforms. These are the states that joined the EU and NATO in 2004 (or later for Bulgaria and Romania). For the new states in the former Yugoslavia and Soviet Union (barring the Baltic States), the transition was not a process of democratization so much as state-building, in some cases nation-building, and often state-capture. Yet, states in all three sub-regions were able to come to a consensus about the institutionalization of the conference into an organization.

Many of these institutions have come back to haunt many governments in the former Soviet Union. Of these, the Russian Federation is the largest, most powerful and influential in the post-Soviet region. Moscow currently leads the group of participating states that is trying to reform the OSCE away from domestic intrusion by the very same institutions that it helped to create years before. The current situation begs two questions: Why was Russian willing to allow the development of the OSCE in this way? What has changed? To start with, Boris Yeltsin's political position was being constantly challenged following Russia's independence, particularly by the communists in the Russian State Duma. With the West being a strong supporter of Yeltsin, both he and the CSCE were keen to see institutions that would ensure Yeltsin remained in power. For the West, however, Yeltsin was seen as the ticket to a democratic Russia, although history has not necessarily played out in this way. For the Russian government, a stronger CSCE would mean "locking in" domestic institutions that would favor the Yeltsin regime. In Moscow, the political opportunities were favorable to deepening in the CSCE.

Second, let us not forget that the relationship between Moscow and the West was rather different in the early 1990s. The West had lent and given Moscow substantial financial support for market reforms and development projects. Third, Moscow saw an opportunity to invest in a new OSCE to replace not only the CSCE generally but also to replace NATO as the primary security organization in the Euro-Atlantic area. An OSCE with institutions and mechanisms to deal with challenges to security would eventually supplant the position of NATO.[46] The fact that this has not happened indicates a substantial misperception of the Yeltsin government and spectacular failure of a key foreign policy objective. Fourth, the Russian Federation was keen to see an institution that would take perceived discrimination against Russian-speakers outside of Russia seriously.[47] For example, the Yeltsin government was able to internationalize the status of Russian-speakers in the Baltic States through the new CSCE bodies, in the same way that the Baltic States were able to use the CSCE to internationalize the continued presence of Russian troops in their countries.[48] Interestingly, both sides tried to claim that their own affairs were outside that of a multi-national organization, claiming that their affairs were either bilateral (in the case of Russia) or domestic (in the case of the Baltic States). Finally, the Helsinki Final Act recognizes the status of current borders. In the early 1990s, many analysts in and outside Russia were unsure about where the breakdown of the Soviet Union would stop. Questions such as what would be the status of Tatarstan or Dagestan in or out of the Russian Federation were common. Thus, the Russian government had an interest in making an organization that recognized the current status of borders. This interest only became more important after the conflict in Chechnya began in December 1994.

So, why have relations changed? M. Steven Fish argues that natural resources such as natural gas and petroleum have changed circumstances in the domestic and international arena.[49] Russia is no longer dependent on Western financial support. The previous asymmetric relationship between Russia and the West is no longer so unbalanced, especially in terms of European relations with Russia. Second, Yeltsin was able to pass on a rather secure presidential role to Vladimir Putin who has made the presidency even more powerful and the Russian state more centralized. Thus, an international actor like the OSCE is no longer required to ensure that institutions are "locked-in" to support the regime. Rather, the OSCE has become more critical of the Russian government over its elections, regional "peace-keepers" and general role in the former Soviet area. The OSCE is not "locking in" regimes that are favorable to the Putin regime, but is an important actor behind the "colored revolutions" in the region. Finally, Russian optimism has dissipated. The OSCE seems to be only focused on disrupting its own interests in the region, NATO survives and has even enlarged despite Russian criticism, while the EU shields the Baltic States from Moscow's complaints about the treatment of Russian-speakers in Estonia and Latvia. Where the OSCE is concerned, political opportunities in Moscow today do not exist.

Conclusion

The transition from "Conference" to "Organization" is an interesting case study in the development and institutionalization of an international organization. The CSCE began to alter to deal with the challenges of the post-Cold War era immediately with the first meetings on the human dimension in 1989 and the subsequent Charter of Paris in 1990, which established the OSCE's key institutions such as the Secretariat and what would become ODIHR. Transition continued with the Helsinki and Stockholm Documents in 1992 that created more institutions such as the HCNM. Eventually, the Budapest Summit in 1994 saw the transition granted with a renaming, from a "Conference on" to an "Organization for." Since the creation of the FOM in 1997, the creation of institutions has stopped. However, the OSCE continues to change with the addition of new roles for current institutions. The transition from "Conference" to "Organization" is important for our study of the OSCE. Let us turn now to see the OSCE in action.

4   Security Management

The OSCE is first and foremost aimed at preventing and managing conflict. While it has other foci, all the institutions, even those seemingly aimed at other issue-areas, are involved in security management. As we see from the discussion of the Final Act in Chapter 2, Baskets II (economic and environmental) and III (human) were directly related to Basket I (politico-military). In this regard, the OSCE's conception of security is based on a comprehensive approach. In his critique of security studies, Johan Galtung advocates casting a wide net when determining the definition of security.[1] More recently, the Copenhagen School has advocated looking at the roots of conflict, which could include societal and human insecurities.[2] This comprehensive approach is that of the OSCE and all of its institutions have something to add to managing security in the Euro-Atlantic area. For example, High Commissioner Rolf Ekeus argues that the HCNM is first and foremost about conflict prevention.[3]

This chapter looks at the OSCE's approach to security management specifically in the areas of the former USSR and Yugoslavia. As stated before, the OSCE's attention is primarily aimed east of Vienna. More specifically, the OSCE has been involved primarily in the collapsed states of the Soviet Union and Yugoslavia. The OSCE remains an important third actor in the four "frozen conflicts" in Transdniestra in Moldova, Nagorno-Karabakh in Azerbaijan as well as Abkhazia and South Ossetia in Georgia. Furthermore, the OSCE has been an early and consistent third actor in the conflicts of the former Yugoslavia. In fact, the first mission was the CSCE Mission to Kosovo, Sandjak and Vojvodina in 1992 to be followed by the CSCE Spillover Monitor Mission to Skopje (FYR Macedonia) the same year. The most recent is the OSCE Mission to Montenegro following its independence from the Republic of Serbia and Montenegro. In all, South-eastern Europe has the greatest concentration of OSCE field missions. In both the former

Soviet Union and Yugoslavia, the aim of the OSCE is conflict prevention, peace, and capacity building.

The focus of the missions in the former Yugoslavia illustrate how
the OSCE has changed from an organization focused on encouraging
security and cooperation between states to the same within states. At
the same time, the OSCE presence in the former Soviet Union and
especially in the Nagorno-Karabakh conflict illustrates how its traditional role still plays a part. In the areas of both collapsed states, the
international plays a large part in the domestic. This chapter focuses
on how the OSCE has attempted to manage security in the Euro-
Atlantic area. The chapter pays particular attention to the former
Soviet Union and Yugoslavia. Furthermore, it is important to keep in
mind that the OSCE does not operate within a vacuum but is instead
part of the European Security Architecture. Therefore, we will also
discuss the OSCE's relationship with other institutions such as the EU,
NATO, and the UN. First, we look in more detail at the mechanisms
of security management. Second, we look at OSCE operations and
treatments in the two collapsed states. We pay particular attention to
several cases: Nagorno-Karabakh, Georgia, and Moldova in the
former Soviet Union and Croatia, Kosovo, and Serbia in the former
Yugoslavia. Finally, we look at the politics of security management in
the OSCE as well as the larger geopolitical implications of the nature
of security management "east of Vienna."

Mechanisms of security management

As discussed, the OSCE approach to security in general is that of
"common and comprehensive" security. Two authors shed light on the
relationship between common and comprehensive security. According
to Jonathan Cohen, in the OSCE, "comprehensive security is matched
by a cooperative [or common] security policy which aims at preventing
emerging conflicts from escalating, emphasizing improved predictability
by increased openness and transparency."[4] Elisa Niemtzow defines
common security as a regime that "functions through agreement on
common goals, norms, and procedures, thus making coercive measures
or the use of physical force unnecessary. [Common or cooperative
security] implies that security is indivisible, in that it is of a global, or
comprehensive nature."[5] For both Cohen and Niemtzow, the relationship between common security, on the one hand, and comprehensive
security on the other, is intrinsic. As argued in Chapter 1, this
approach to security is what makes the OSCE different from other
security institutions in the region. While NATO has taken on a

broader security agenda, it remains primarily concerned with traditional threats to security. The EU also has a broad security agenda but this too is dominated by traditional power politics and so-called "positive power."[6] The Council of Europe is limited in its scope when it comes to security, primarily concentrating on human security as it pertains to democracy, democratization, and human rights. Only the OSCE has a common and comprehensive security agenda.

"Common and comprehensive" security was originally designed for mediating the Cold War in Europe. Since the end of the Cold War, however, the challenges of common and comprehensive security have been three-fold.[7] First, the OSCE was tasked with providing for a security regime that would offer Russia an institutionalized say in European security.[8] As discussed in Chapter 3, Russia was keen to see the OSCE surpass NATO as the key security institution in the Eurasian region. The decision to further enlarge NATO in 2002 put an end to such a policy in Moscow. For NATO's part, the organization did bring Russia onto the NATO-Russia Council, but this is hardly a replacement for "an institutionalized say in European security." Second, as previously discussed, the OSCE had to come to grips with collapsing states in the USSR and Yugoslavia. Events in the Balkans and the Caucasus were already in a bad state before the OSCE was able to develop instruments to engage such crises such as the long-term missions. Third, the OSCE was required to develop an instrument to engage problems over national minorities. The HCNM was developed in response to this need. While we have seen developments in other areas of concern such as organized crime and terrorism, the mechanisms of security management are devoted to these three tasks.

The OSCE has attempted to manage the insecurities of the post-Cold War era by developing five mechanisms.[9] First, the OSCE has tied the human dimension to long-term conflict prevention by promoting democratization and human rights. The focus on human rights was an important part of the Final Act, as we saw in Chapter 2. However, the focus on democracy and democratization has come about since the end of the Cold War, beginning with the first human dimension meeting in Paris in May–June 1989. Long-term conflict prevention was further developed in the 1990 Paris Charter for a New Europe that created the Office of Free Elections (precursor to ODIHR) and the 1992 Helsinki Document that created the HCNM. Long-term conflict prevention is an important part of the OSCE's tools of managing security. For that reason, it is difficult to take it out of the larger discussion of security management as presented in this chapter. While this chapter does discuss on the first mechanism, we flesh out this aspect of the OSCE in Chapter 5, given the relationship between long-term conflict prevention and human security.

Second, the organization relies on the mechanism of conflict prevention through monitoring and early warning. This second mechanism is spread across institutions in the OSCE such as the FSC, the CPC, and the HCNM. Monitoring and early warnings were part of the CSBMs developed in the Final Act, not to mention the CFE Treaties and Open Skies Treaty. Long- and short-term conflict prevention is a traditional aspect of a common security organization in general and the OSCE specifically. During the Cold War, conflict prevention was key to avoiding a third world war in the Euro-Atlantic area between rival superpowers. However, the potential for conflict has mostly been within states, between the center and periphery or between opposing ethnic groups. The OSCE's transition from conference to organization was a response to these new insecurities of the post-Cold War era. On one hand, the OSCE record on preventing conflict has been limited, especially in the area of the former Yugoslavia. However, many of the conflicts in the OSCE region had begun before the organization had the mechanisms with which to prevent them. Yet, there have been some successful conflict-prevention operations in Estonia, Latvia, and Macedonia, predominantly led by the HCNM but also by OSCE missions to the three states.

Third, the OSCE employs mediation tactics during ceasefire negotiations. For instance, the OSCE was important in bringing about the lasting ceasefire in 1996 between the Russian Federation and the breakaway region of Chechnya.[10] In particular, the so-called OSCE Assistance Group to Chechnya, created in 1995 and led by Ambassador Tom Guldimann, negotiated a ceasefire from inside the battle zone. Despite the eventual reoccurrence of war in 1999, the OSCE-negotiated ceasefire between Alexander Lebed and Zelimkhan Yanderbiev is seen as one of the OSCE's crowning achievements. While the OSCE was an important part of the ceasefire, there are other reasons why the conflict may have come to an end in 1996, including the death (from a Russian bomb) of the Chechen resistance leader Dzhokhar Dudayev and Russian presidential elections the same year.[11] Nevertheless, the OSCE Assistance Group to Chechnya does illustrate that the organization has the capacity to operate effectively in a battle zone and is able to help alleviate conflict.

Fourth, once a ceasefire has been negotiated, the OSCE relies on missions to prevent the reignition of conflict. First, the OSCE ensures that the parties to the agreement hold to the terms of the ceasefire. Often, missions also focus on the underlying reasons for the previous eruption of conflict. Post-negotiated settlement conflict prevention is most strongly evidenced in the "frozen" conflicts of the former Soviet Union and resolved conflicts of the former Yugoslavia. As we see in more detail in this chapter, the OSCE has been an important negotiator and confidence-builder in Nagorno-Karabakh, South Ossetia, and Moldova. Furthermore, post-settlement conflict prevention was also the role of the OSCE in Bosnia-Herzegovina following the Dayton Peace Accords.[12] This fourth mechanism of security management is part of the initial period following the ceasefire. For the "frozen" conflicts, this has been an indefinite stage. However, for the conflicts in the former Yugoslavia, the OSCE's final mechanism has been employed.

The final OSCE security management mechanism is post-conflict security-building. This process goes beyond the point of maintaining that parties are keeping to the conditions of the ceasefire. Instead, post-conflict security building is part of the normalization of political relations following a conflict. In the OSCE's case, this includes state-building, such as in Bosnia where the OSCE has helped organize municipal elections.[13] Indeed, the clearest evidence of post-conflict security-building has been the OSCE work in the former Yugoslavia.[14] Post-conflict security- and state-building is also an area where the organizational overlap is most dense. The OSCE has to collaborate with various international organizations such as the UN, the EU, NATO and the Council of Europe during this phase, not to mention the plethora of NGOs involved. In fact, Charles Krupnick has referred to the OSCE itself as an "intergovernmental NGO" based on the way it works in the region.[15] This NGO-side of the OSCE will be discussed in more detail in the following chapter, with the focus on democratization and human rights. Overall, the OSCE has had an important impact on security management in the Euro-Atlantic region. We can see how these mechanisms have been employed by looking at how the OSCE has responded to conflict in the former Soviet Union and Yugoslavia.

Managing state collapse

Of the five mechanisms of security management, the OSCE has primarily engaged the final two: ceasefire monitoring and post-conflict security-building. Few conflicts have broken out since the early years of the post-Cold War era. For example, of our six case studies, only the Kosovo conflict began after the 1992 Stockholm and Helsinki Documents which established OSCE missions and other security management institutions. Due to the early advent of conflict, it makes sense that the majority of the OSCE work in security management can be characterized by the last two mechanisms. In other words, many of the changes in the OSCE that occurred in the transition from conference to organization were in response to many of the case studies we discuss in this chapter. In order to show the OSCE in terms of managing security, we focus on the former Soviet Union and Yugoslavia. In the former Soviet Union, we look at OSCE participation in the "frozen conflicts" of Nagorno-Karabakh in Azerbaijan, South Ossetia in Georgia, and Moldova. In the former Yugoslavia, we look at the OSCE missions to Croatia, Kosovo, and Serbia. In all the case studies, intra-state ethnic conflict was the nature of the unrest. Where the Soviet Union simply dissolved, Yugoslavia fractured asunder. Thus, it is ironic that the conflicts in the former Soviet Union remain "frozen" while the conflicts in the former Yugoslavia have ceased and peace- and state-building has begun. We shall see that this irony is largely explained by one single factor: the Russian Federation. We ask two questions in the following case studies. How has the OSCE been able to cope with conflict in Russia's "near abroad"? What role has the OSCE played in managing state-collapse and state-building following the end of the "Greater Serbia" project?

Nagorno-Karabakh

The conflict in Nagorno-Karabakh is the closest we come to inter-state conflict in the OSCE region. Like many conflicts in the former Socialist bloc, there are many dimensions to the "frozen" conflict in Nagorno-Karabakh. There are two immediate actors: Azerbaijan and the Armenians living in the mountainous region of Nagorno-Karabakh. Perhaps sensing eventual Armenian independence, the Nagorno-Karabakh Armenians voted to separate from the Azerbaijani SSR and join the Armenian SSR in 1988. Neither the Soviet nor Azerbaijani authorities recognized the vote nor did either recognize the irredentist tendencies of the mountainous enclave. In 1991 as the Soviet Union began to break apart, Nagorno-Karabakh changed track and declared outright independence from Azerbaijan, leaving aside becoming part of Armenia. The Azerbaijani authorities responded with force to stop the breakaway enclave. The conflict lasted for three years and eventually a ceasefire was negotiated in May 1994.

The crisis in Nagorno-Karabakh is international in nature. For Rogers Brubaker, competing nationalisms are likely to form when there is a nationalizing majority (in this case, the Azerbaijanis), a nationalizing minority community (Armenians in Nagorno-Karabakh), and an external national homeland (the Armenian state).[16] As Map 4.1 illustrates, the Nagorno-Karabakh enclave is near the Armenian border with Azerbaijan, although not contiguous with it. While officially remaining neutral, groups within the Armenian state, including the military, were supporting the secessionist movement. Armenian support for the enclave is based partly on a perception of historical oppression from Turks, to which the great majority of Azerbaijanis belong. Also, the conflict is a result of Soviet internal borders. Armenians both inside and out of the Armenian SSR argued in Soviet times for the inclusion of Nagorno-Karabakh in the Armenian rather than the Azerbaijani side. The conflict is complex for these are only two of many historical legacies which impact on current events in the enclave.

The conflict was made even more complex by the participation of the Russian Federation, as supporters of the then newly formed Armenian state, and of Turkey, as traditional supporters of Turkish peoples in the Caucasus and Central Asia.[17] Note that all the states involved are members of the OSCE. Turkey has supported the

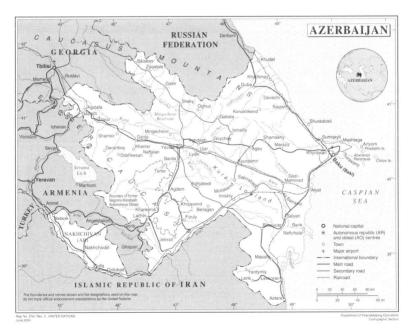

Map 4.1 Azerbaijan.

Source: UN Cartographic Section, No. 3761 Rev. 5 January 2004.

Azerbaijani state but had little impact on the conflict. On the other hand, Russia has been a key actor in the conflict, ceasefire, and subsequent peace-keeping. While Russia has been instrumental in bringing peace to the region, it has also maintained the status quo of a "frozen" conflict. This dual nature of the Russian influence will be seen in the cases of South Ossetia and Moldova as well. Nevertheless, as a key actor in the region Russia matters for both cooperation and conflict. Furthermore, while Russia is a part of the ongoing negotiations known as the Minsk Group, it remains skeptical of the efforts of the outside community in undermining its interests in the region. While we have not seen large-scale conflict since 1994, the conflict remains "frozen." The OSCE has been an important "third-party" actor from the beginning.

OSCE involvement in the Nagorno-Karabakh crisis began in 1992, once the two nations became participating-states in the CSCE.[18] The Council of Ministers mandated that a conference be established to seek out peaceful solutions to the conflict.[19] This conference was located in Minsk, the Belarussian capital. The conference participants were Belarus, Denmark, Finland, France, Germany, Italy, Poland, Russia, Sweden, Turkey, and the United States as well as Armenia and Azerbaijan. Note that the Armenians from Nagorno-Karabakh do not have a position in the Minsk group, a point that the Armenian government has attempted to change without success. Perhaps misperceiving the conflict as overly simplistic, a point expressed by Terhi Hakala, the conference turned into a working group subsequently known as the Minsk Process, which includes the same members together known as the Minsk group.[20] The complex and international dimension of the Nagorno-Karabakh crisis makes it an unfortunate test-case for the early post-Cold War CSCE. Since 1992, the Minsk Process has rumbled on without resolving the conflict but nevertheless making conflict less likely.

In addition to the attending countries, the Minsk Process has four important institutional actors. First, the 1994 Budapest Summit (where the CSCE became the OSCE) added to the Minsk Process with the establishment of the "Co-Chairman of the Minsk Process." The 1996 Lisbon Summit subsequently altered the Co-Chairmanship to consist of a troika consisting of the US, France, and the Russian Federation. Second, the CiO established a Personal Representative on the Minsk Conference in 1995. Andrzej Kasprzyk of Poland has been the Co-Chairman since January 1997. In general, the Personal Representative is a liaison between the CiO and the Minsk Process as well as between the OSCE and other international organizations operating in the region, such as the UN. While the CiO changes once a year, institutional memory remains with the Co-Chairman. Third, the OSCE High Level Planning Group (HLPG) was created in 1994 to coordinate prospective peace-keeping operations. The new institution replaced the pre-existing Initial Operations Planning Group. The HLPG consists of military attaches seconded by participating-states. Not all participating-states will have the need and/or ability to send a military expert to the HLPG. While the HLPG has planned for an OSCE multinational peacekeeping force in Nagorno-Karabakh, Armenia and the Russian Federation have been reluctant to cede changes to the current peacekeeping force of the Commonwealth of Independent States (CIS) in the region. Finally, the Minsk Process is helped by the OSCE offices in Yerevan and Baku, the Armenian and Azerbaijani capitals respectively. The offices were created in 1999 and 2000 respectively by an act of the PC, following the acceptance for missions by the respective governments. The aims of the missions are broader than the Minsk Process, but lend to the objective of peace and security in the region.

Initially, the OSCE appeared to have an important impact on the conflict. The 1994 ceasefire was negotiated between the Russian Federation and the OSCE. According to Hakala, the OSCE Minsk Process was undermined from early on because some actors sought alternatives to the OSCE peace-process.[21] Furthermore, numerous actors were involved in addition to the OSCE, including the UN Security Council and the UNHCR. The multitude of actors in addition to the lack of cohesion in the Minsk group meant that actors to the conflict could shop around for the mediator that best suited their interest. Nevertheless, the peace process began in 1994 with an OSCE-sponsored settlement. There is little doubt that the mandate to issue peacekeepers under the auspices of the OSCE had an impact on the settlement. The decision to give the OSCE the ability to issue its own peacekeepers came about at the 1994 Budapest Summit. While there have been numerous unarmed observers across the OSCE region, there has yet to be an occasion where OSCE peacekeepers have been deployed.

The task of the Minsk Process has been to bring a lasting settlement to Nagorno-Karabakh and, as we have seen, competing interests from all sides make this difficult. There have been two strategies of the Minsk Process: the "package" solution and the "step-by-step" solution.[22] The earlier approach was the "package" solution whereby a lasting settlement would arise from complex simultaneous process of granting autonomy to Nagorno-Karabakh, withdrawing Nagorno-Karabakh forces from the six occupied regions of Azerbaijan, and demilitarizing the conflict area. Such an approach has been used in other post-conflict situations particularly after peace-keepers have arrived, such as in the case of Bosnia. Needless to say, the positions of Nagorno-Karabakh and Armenia on one side and Azerbaijan on the other were too far apart for any "package" to go ahead.

Following the creation of the Minsk Troika, there was a transition towards the "step-by-step" solution, which has been favored by the Azerbaijani and Armenians, although not the leadership in Nagorno-Karabakh. The first step would be the withdrawal of Nagorno-Karabakh forces from other areas of Azerbaijan surrounding Nagorno-Karabakh, but particularly those areas connecting Armenia to the enclave. Until the withdrawal happens, the status of the enclave is officially off the agenda of the Minsk group. The Azerbaijani government has offered the breakaway enclave so-called internal self-determination that would offer considerable autonomy to Nagorno-Karabakh within Azerbaijan. Similarly, the OSCE has been inclined to support an internal solution that does not disrupt the territorial status quo. This has led some to question the "third party" nature of the organization.[23] Nevertheless, the OSCE is committed to territorial integrity both in general according to the Helsinki Final Act and specifically in the case of Nagorno-Karabakh as seen in the Hungarian CiO decisions in 1995. However, there is a political will within the organization to keep Azerbaijan whole and otherwise happy because of its oil and gas reserves. At the same time, as can be seen in the case of the referendum for Montenegrin independence in 2006, the OSCE's commitment to territorial integrity is not always consist. Nevertheless, while all parties to the conflict have an interest in keeping it "frozen" and thus largely peaceful, the difficulty will be getting a lasting resolution.

South Ossetia

The "frozen" conflict in South Ossetia is different than that of Nagorno-Karabakh because, while Ossetians live on both sides of the Russian-Georgian border, there is no external national homeland to support the South Ossetians. At the same time, the "frozen" conflicts, including that of Moldova, are similar in that Russia plays a part in not only "keeping the peace" but also in protecting the interests of the breakaway enclave. Georgia's post-Soviet relationship with Russia has been strained from the beginning partly because the Georgian leadership consolidated power by withdrawing from links with the Russian Federation as quickly as possible, as did the Baltic States.[24] Similar to the Baltic experiences, the process of state-building accompanied nation-building.[25] As Georgia struggled for a centripetal sense of

"Georgianness," internal and external actors felt the centrifugal impact of nation-building. Georgia experienced two large-scale conflicts, in Abkhazia and South Ossetia. Both enclaves have attempted to secede from Georgia (Map 4.2). The Abkhaz leadership has struggled for outright independence, while the South Ossetians have declared their intention to join with the Russian federal state of North Ossetia. Furthermore, the Abkhaz conflict has been on a greater scale than that of South Ossetia. Nevertheless, Abkhazia does not come under the remit of the OSCE where the UN remains the dominant international organization, although the OSCE did participate in the UN-led negotiations from 1994.[26] The focus of the OSCE has been firmly on the conflict in South Ossetia.

The OSCE became involved with the conflicts in Georgia following an invitation by the Georgian government in 1992 to act as mediator in Abkhazia and South Ossetia. The PC responded by creating the mandate for the OSCE Mission to Georgia which began in November 1992. The mission was mandated to promote a lasting settlement in Georgia specifically and South Ossetia particularly.[27] Furthermore, the

Map 4.2 Georgia.

Source: UN Cartographic Section, No. 3780 Rev. 5 August 2004.

OSCE mission to Georgia was aimed at promoting democratization and human rights in post-Soviet Georgia. The invitation of the Georgian government followed the Sochi Agreement in June 1992 which consisted of a ceasefire, the creation of the Joint Control Commission and the Joint Peacekeeping Forces Group. The peace-keeping force was and remains under Russian military command, although Georgian and North Ossetian troops also participate in the peacekeeping arrangements. The initial OSCE mission mandate was to monitor these peacekeeping forces.

The mandate of the OSCE Mission to Georgia has been subsequently expanded. This wider mandate has allowed the OSCE to work on a "step-by-step" basis in finding a solution to the "frozen" conflict in South Ossetia similar to the Minsk group approach to Nagorno-Karabakh. The mission is engaged with developing a broader political framework that leads to a final resolution of the conflict.[28] The mission also immersed itself in the institutions arranged by the Sochi Agreement. For instance, the mission has been set to monitor the ceasefire and peacekeeping forces. Furthermore, the OSCE is engaged through the mission with the Joint Control Commission to facilitate cooperation between parties to the conflict. Finally, the OSCE has a presence at the local level in the conflict region by remaining in contact with local authorities. In 1997, the OSCE and UN signed a Memorandum of Understanding that allowed the OSCE to support the UN Human Rights Office in Abkhazia, where at least one OSCE officer has been working since. Moreover, since the re-ignition in 1999 of conflict in Chechnya, located next to South Ossetia, the mission was expanded to monitor the Georgian-Russian border. There was considerable concern in Moscow that Chechen fighters were using South Ossetia as a base and that weapons and other resources were coming through its territory. The border monitoring mission appears to have ended in June 2004 due to a failure of the Permanent Council (PC) to renew the expanded mandate. However, in April 2005, the PC instructed the OSCE mission to Georgia to begin a border guard training program. As alluded to earlier, the role of the mission has been to support nation-building through de-securitizing the region. Despite the OSCE's intent, the conflict in South Ossetia, as in Abkhazia, remains "frozen."

The role of the OSCE as a peace-maker was made both easier and more difficult after the Rose Revolution in 2003.[29] President Mikhail Saakashvili has been keen to engage with Western organizations and support democratization efforts in Georgia. At the same time, having solved the regional dispute over the Ajara region, he has promised to do the same in South Ossetia, making the Ossetian leadership concerned about a possible escalation.[30] Saakashvili has also demanded that Russian peacekeepers in South Ossetia and Abkhazia be replaced by a multinational force, to which Moscow has given a cold response. Incidentally, the terms of the Adapted CFE Treaty (Istanbul Summit 1999) stipulate a replacement of Russian forces in Georgia (as well as the other "frozen" conflicts in the region). Overall, the OSCE, as well as the EU and NATO, is keen to see Georgia maintain its borders. The solution for South Ossetia specifically will lie with specially arranged internal self-determination. However, the Russian military presence in the region means that this solution will be further delayed.

Transdniestra

The Transdniestrian conflict is the first case study in this book that deals with "Russians beyond Russia."[31] The conflict in Moldova was the result also of simultaneous nation- and state-building projects.[32] At the beginning of the twentieth century, Moldova (known at the time as Bessarabia) was part of the Russian Empire. But with the advent of the Russian Civil War in 1918, Moldova declared independence from Russia and became part of greater Romania. Moldova was then annexed to the Soviet Union in 1944, similar to the Baltic Republics (see Map 4.3). At the break-up of the Soviet Union, Moldova gained its independence. Moldovan culture and language are to all intents and purposes Romanian, despite a long period of Russification during the Soviet Period.[33] As Georgia was discovering what it meant to be Georgian, so Moldova was discovering what it meant to be Moldovan. The leadership in Chisinau, the Moldovan capital, discovered that to be Moldovan was to be Romanian. Even before the end of Soviet rule, there had been local efforts to return the Moldovan language to Latin script as well as make Moldovan the official state language. The efforts succeeded. The minority community, primarily in the Transdniestrian region, and primarily consisting of Russian-speakers, resented the nation-building project. Up to this point, events in Moldova had been nearly identical to the nationalist movements in Estonia and Latvia. However, a key difference was the potential for reunification with the external homeland of the Moldovans, a crucial difference between the Baltic and Moldovan experiences. According to Maria Raquel Freire, the promotion of Moldovan and virtual relegation of Russian led the Transdniestrians to think that Moldova was headed towards reunification with Romania.[34] Following a declaration of independence for the "Moldovan Transdniestrian Republic," the tension escalated to open conflict in 1992.

Map 4.3 Moldova.

Source: UN Cartographic Section, No. 3759 Rev. 2 January 2004.

Soviet and then Russian troops remained in Moldova after the dissolution of the Soviet Union in 1991. In particular, the Russian 14th Army
remained in the Transdniestrian region. With Russian military assistance,
the Transdniestrian forces were able to overcome "poorly equipped
Moldovan police and ill-trained armed forces."[35] On the "left bank," the
Russian 14th Army equipped and instructed the Transdniestrian side.

The initial fighting was fierce and in the end, the Moldovan forces withdrew from the breakaway region several months after the initial clashes. Tellingly, the Moldovan government and the Russian Federation signed a ceasefire agreement in July 1992. The agreement actually transformed Russia's role in the conflict to that of third party. The ceasefire arrangements took similar shape to those of the Sochi Agreement that settled the conflict in South Ossetia with the establishment of a Joint Control Commission subordinated to a Trilateral Joint Military Command. The key difference between the Transdniestrian and Sochi agreements is that Transdniestrian forces were officially allowed to be a part of the peacekeeping forces. South Ossetians were not allowed to take part in peacekeeping, although some did participate through the North Ossetian battalions.

From the start of hostilities, the Moldovans requested that the UN and OSCE become involved in mediation. At the request of the Moldovan government, a CSCE rapporteur visit took place in March 1992.[36] Nevertheless, as discussed earlier in this chapter, the mechanisms to manage insecurities in the OSCE region were only created at the Helsinki Summit in July 1992. The conflict had erupted and abated by the time the OSCE could respond on a large scale. By the time that the OSCE was able to fully respond, the Moldovan government had lost more territory to the separatists and Russia was the key broker to the conflict, despite being a party to the early fighting. Eventually, an OSCE mission to Moldova was established in February 1993. Considering the "frozen" nature of the conflict, the OSCE mission mandate has remained consistent. As in the cases of other OSCE missions in conflict zones, there are three core objectives: peace-building, state-building and promoting the human dimension. According to the organization, the OSCE mission to Moldova works closely with the Joint Constitutional Commission, which includes both the Moldovans and the Transdniestrians.[37] The commission is part of the OSCE's efforts to produce a political framework to resolve the conflict. In connection to the peace efforts, the OSCE mission monitors the military situation in the region. Most recently, the 1999 Istanbul Summit mandated that a fund be established to allow the mission to monitor the removal and destruction of Russian ammunition and armaments. Also, the OSCE mission has been supporting the development of democratic institutions and insuring the protection of human rights. Particular attention has been paid to the role of the media in Moldova in conjunction with the FOM as well as the trafficking of human beings in conjunction with ODIHR.

While the OSCE has been working towards resolving the "frozen" conflict in the Transdniestrian region, little progress has been made since the Adapted CFE Treaty mandated that Russian troops be withdrawn from the area to be replaced by multinational forces. Many in the organization see Russia as being the key to resolving the conflict, but also the promoter of the status quo. Russian officials argue that the intransigence lies with the Transdniestrians rather than the Russian government.[38] In essence, the Transdniestrian leadership has refused to permit the Russian government from withdrawing troops. If such is the case, it raises serious questions of Moscow's influence over an otherwise small actor in an otherwise small state.

On the part of the OSCE, the CPC, on behalf of the FSC, has a route to resolving the conflict with or without the withdrawal of Russian troops. Despite the general differences and local nuances of the three "frozen" conflicts that we have discussed thus far, the CPC plan to solve the Transdniestrian conflict could be generally transposed onto the conflicts in Georgia and Azerbaijan. According to advisors in the CPC, there are several steps to resolving the conflict.[39] First, the OSCE would like to see a common customs arrangement between the state of Moldova and the Transdniestrian region. Mutual prosperity and trading should encourage confidence and security. Second, there needs to be monitoring of the arms manufactures in Transdniestra. The making of small arms is not only a problem for the Transdniestrian case but also for conflicts further afield, including outside the OSCE area.

Third, the CPC would like to see an increased transparency in the exchange of military information between the state, the breakaway region and third parties. Transparency and information exchange are traditional CSBMs in the OSCE catalogue. Fourth, there needs to be a realization by the Moldovan authorities that the Transdniestrian region will require special status *within* the state of Moldova. Fifth, Russia remains a vital supplier of arms and ammunition to the Transdniestrians. Thus, a lasting peace settlement will require Russia to withdraw these services from the breakaway region. Finally, the Moldovans need to cease participating in the ceasefire agreement signed between it and the Russian Federation in 1992. Rather, Moldova should seek instead to fit within an OSCE peace settlement. The current settlement forces the government of Moldova to follow the terms and conditions set by the Russian Federation. Overall, Russia's ability to shape the "frozen" conflicts has had an unfortunate impact on the ability to find a lasting peace. While the Russian government has sought to bring peace and stability to the region, it has done so with its own foreign policy interests in mind. The sooner Russia withdraws troops and supplies in the "frozen" conflicts as mandated by the Istanbul Summit, the sooner the regions will find a lasting peace settlement.

Croatia

The conflict in the former Yugoslavia is different in scale and impact than those in the former Soviet Union. As Yugoslavia began to break apart, first Slovenia, then Croatia, nationalism mixed with ethnic intolerance to create the conditions for open, widespread conflict not seen in Europe since the Second World War.[40] As Salmon has shown, the conflict in the former Yugoslavia challenged the very essence of European political cooperation.[41] In the end, it was the Euro-Atlantic area that came together to address the conflict, first under the auspices of the UN and eventually NATO.[42] Recent history in the West has shown the Serbians to be aggressors in the Yugoslav conflicts. However, this interpretation ignores those Serbs who suffered under the Slobodan Milošević regime as well as those who were themselves "cleansed" from Croatian, Bosnian, and Albanian territories.[43] Nor should we ignore the aggression of the Yugoslav government in the name of a greater Serbia. The Serb violence against the Bosniak population is the best known. However, Croatia under Franjo Tuđman was a co-aggressor with the Milošević regime in cleansing areas of Bosniaks. Thus, not only did Croatia fight its own war of independence against the Yugoslav government but also tried to carve a piece of Croatia out of Bosnia-Herzegovina through ethnic cleansing before then joining with the Bosnians to fight against the Yugoslav Army. The official end to the fighting came with the Dayton Peace Accords in November 1995. The irony for Serb and Croatian nationalists is that ethnic cleansing on their part would eventually lead to the ethnic cleansing of Serbs and Croatians from some Bosnian and Kosovo Albanian territories.

Croatia's path to peace was difficult but helped along by its geographic location. Just south from Austria and set across the Adriatic Sea from Italy (Map 4.4), Croatia's potential to impact Western Europe was quickly recognized. Croatia had to cope with controlling nationalist tendencies following a violent conflict where there were both aggressors and victims. The part of any international organization was to manage nation-building and create a functioning democratic state, while Croatia dealt with new national minorities with external national homelands and thousands of displaced persons from Bosnia. Super power politics also played a part in the former Yugoslavia and Croatia, but not quite the same way as in our case studies in the former Soviet Union. Russia was an ally of the Yugoslav government, but eventually cajoled Milošević to attend the Dayton Peace Conference.[44] At the same time, the United States was key in bringing the Croatian and Bosniak-Croatian forces to the negotiating table. The Dayton

Peace Accords brought a lasting peace to Croatia and Bosnia (and temporarily to the remainder of Yugoslavia). Thus, a "frozen" conflict in the region was avoided. Following the peace settlement, it was time for the makers, keepers, and builders of peace: international organizations. The entire Yugoslav area has been overloaded with international organizations such as the UN, NATO, the EU, and the Council of Europe. Within this myriad of international organizations, the OSCE has played an important part.

The OSCE Mission to Croatia was established by the PC in April 1996. The mission mandate contains four objectives to promote confidence and security in Croatia.[45] First, the OSCE mission provided assistance to state and local authorities regarding the treatment of national minorities, primarily Serbs who live near the border with Serbia. Croatia's number of minorities fell sharply during the wars with Bosnia and Yugoslavia. Nevertheless, the treatment of the remaining Serb population was particularly important during the Milošević years (1989–2000) where discrimination could have produced further conflict with Yugoslavia. The mission's concentration on

Map 4.4 Croatia.

Source: UN Cartographic Section, no. 3740 Rev. 5 January 2004.

national minorities overlaps with the mandate of the HCNM. Second, the OSCE mission was to support state-building. The OSCE was particularly interested in promoting democratic institutions as a method for post-conflict reconciliation. The concentration on democratic institutions also involves the work of ODIHR. Third, the mission mandate was later expanded to deal with the problem of refugees and displaced persons. In this regard, the mission has worked with the UNHCR and various NGOs.[46] Finally, the mission was on the ground to relay information to the PC and Secretariat. As we have stated before, the on-the-ground information gathering and monitoring of the missions is one of the greatest assets of the OSCE.

At the time of writing, Croatia has moved beyond its earlier post-conflict status. Croatia is considered to be a democratic state that by and large protects human and minority rights. The government continues to work with the International Criminal Tribunal for the Former Yugoslavia. Finally, Croatia has been a candidate country for EU membership since October 2005. While the OSCE has not been able to match the financial contributions of the EU in its PHARE program or its large body of administrative expertise serviced through the twinning program, the OSCE has played an important part in bringing Croatia to this stage. The OSCE has continued to concentrate on their strengths, including building confidence and security, promoting democratic institutions, and human rights, as well as protecting national minorities.

Kosovo

Events in the southern Yugoslav state of Kosovo (Map 4.5) were both the beginning and end of the project for a greater Serbia. Kosovo plays a special role in the Serb psyche. In particular, the infamous Battle of Kosovo in 1389 was where Prince Lazar rallied Serbs *and* Bosnians to fight against the Ottoman invasion. The Serb-Bosnian coalition was eventually defeated and Prince Lazar went down in Serb historiography as a blessed martyr for the fight against the Ottomans in Europe. There was a traditional presence of Serbs in Kosovo before and since the battle. At the same time, there was also a traditional presence of Albanians, with the state of Albania to the South. As ethnonationalism was building in Yugoslavia, competing Albanian and Serbian nationalisms in Kosovo became increasingly violent. In the early 1980s, the Kosovo Serb population experienced considerable hostility from the Kosovo Albanian community. Later in 1989, on the 600th anniversary of the Battle of Kosovo, it was in the name of a

Map 4.5 Kosovo region.

Source: UN Cartographic Section, No. 4069 Rev. 2 January 2004.

Serbian Kosovo that Milošević changed from being a socialist techno-crat to a nationalist autocrat and eventual warlord.

At the beginning of the Yugoslav conflict, the key battle zones were Bosnia, Serbia, and Croatia. At this time, the conflict in Kosovo was far less violent and less organized. Kosovo was spared the initial conflict because Belgrade was focused on Bosnia and Croatia. Thus, when the Dayton Peace Accords were signed in 1995, the official Yugoslav forces withdrew from Bosnia-Herzegovina. Following the Dayton Peace Accords, Albanian nationalists both within Kosovo and from Albania itself were beginning their fight against Yugoslavia in the name of the Kosovo Liberation Army (KLA). With the wars lost with Croatia, then Bosnia, the project for a greater Albania with its sights on the very place that Serbian culture considered holy became the next conflict. With these three conflicts in mind, it is important to stress that Serb leaders always considered their violent actions to be in defense of Serbs living in multi-ethnic communities who were being discriminated against, such as the aggression against Kosovo Serbs in the early 1980s. Thus, with an authoritarian nationalist government in Yugoslavia, Serb nationalism came to meet Albanian nationalism in open conflict.

Open conflict between the regular Yugoslav forces and the KLA began shortly after the Yugoslav withdrawal from Bosnia. There was a considerable difference in the means to wage a campaign between the two sides. The Yugoslav army was better equipped with soldiers and fire power. Due to the asymmetry, the KLA operated as a guerrilla force. The very fact that the KLA chose to use guerrilla tactics meant that distinguishing between civilian and combatant was difficult for the Serbians. Thus, anti-Albanian violence was often indiscriminate. Coupled with a Serbian perception of a right to Kosovo as well as general Serbian nationalism, the result was lethal for the Kosovo Albanian civilian community. The violence caused thousands of displaced persons. Milošević was forced to sign a ceasefire agreement in 1998, but was later perceived to have violated the agreement conditions. After meeting in February/March 1999, NATO began an air campaign to force Yugoslavia to withdraw from Kosovo.[47] Official NATO targets included Yugoslav military units in Kosovo as well as logistics in Serbia proper, such as communications centers, electricity stations, and bridges. NATO bombing caused thousands of Serbs to flee the area. Intensive air bombardment led in months to a NATO-led peacekeeping force, KFOR. In the end, Kosovo has been "cleansed" of the majority of Serbs who formerly lived there.

OSCE participation in Kosovo began in 1992 with the deployment of the OSCE Mission to Kosovo, Sandjak, and Vojvodina. The mission only lasted until April 1993, as the Yugoslav government rejected any further extension. This followed the decision by the CSO (early PC) in 1992 to suspend Yugoslavia from the OSCE altogether, based on the "consensus-minus-one" rule. The OSCE returned again in the OSCE Kosovo Verification Mission that sent OSCE monitors to observe the ceasefire agreement of 1998.[48] The monitoring ended with the violent reengagement of Yugoslav and KLA forces. The OSCE returned a third time in the post-conflict phase with the OSCE mission to Kosovo in July 1999 which works within the United Nations Interim Administration Mission in Kosovo (UNMIK). The mission takes the lead role within UNMIK in matters relating to "human resources capacity, institution building, and human rights."[49] Human resource capacity building is primarily aimed at supporting the Kosovo police service through the Kosovo Police School, established and operated by the OSCE mission to Kosovo. The mission is also working on the construction of democratic institutions in Kosovo, including supporting the positive development of civil society.[50] Finally, the mission is working with the UNHCR to support human and minority rights in Kosovo.[51] Thus far, the status of Kosovo still remains unclear. Currently Kosovo is administered by the UN through UNMIK. The leadership in Kosovo has stated that it will accept nothing less than independence. At the same time, Serbia has demanded an autonomous Kosovo within Serbia. The one option that is not being discussed is the prospect of Kosovo becoming part of Albania.

Serbia

The Yugoslav wars began in 1991 when Slovenia seceded from the Yugoslav Republic. The Yugoslav military responded with force. The same year, Croatia was the next to declare independence from the Yugoslav Republic. Again, the Yugoslav military responded, but Croatia provided a robust defense. In 1992, Bosnia-Herzegovina followed Croatia and declared its independence from the Yugoslav Republic. Once again, the Yugoslav military responded, but this time with brutal violence against Bosnian Muslims. The OSCE saw three acts of aggression by the Yugoslav government. Initially, the organization expressed concern through the CiO, the representative of the CiO, as well as individual participating-state delegations.[52] At the Prague Meeting in January 1992, the OSCE adopted the "consensus-minus-one" mechanism that would allow the PC to take action where there are clear signs that a state is violating the norms as set out in the Final Act and subsequent OSCE decisions. By this point, there was already a realization that the OSCE would not be able to come to a consensus on the Yugoslav conflicts as long as Yugoslavia continued to block decisions. The Yugoslav suspension occurred in two phases. First, the PC took the decision to invoke the "consensus-minus-one" mechanism on 12 May 1992. The main topic of discussion was the Yugoslav violence in Bosnia-Herzegovina. Valery Perry argues that "this initial suspension allowed for the [mechanism] of consensus minus one to be applied specifically in those discussions of issues pertaining to the Yugoslav crises."[53] Second, on 10 July 1992, at the Helsinki Summit, participants decided that Yugoslavia would no longer be able to attend the summit meetings nor any subsequent meetings. The terms of ending the suspension were to allow OSCE missions to resume in the region.[54] The suspension of Yugoslavia meant that the OSCE was able to maneuver around the Yugoslav crisis without the veto of what was basically Serbia and Montenegro. The suspension also meant that the OSCE lost a line of communication with Belgrade and thus had little ability to impact events on the ground.

The OSCE's relationship with what eventually came to be officially Serbia (Map 4.6) and Montenegro changed after the fall of Milošević. Having lost an election but still refusing to relinquish power, the Serbian people mobilized in protests and rallies to bring an end to the regime. The eventual replacement, Vojislav Kostunica, was himself a nationalist but of a different sort to Milošević. Kostunica was quick to attempt to engage with the OSCE. Recognizing this, the PC voted in November 2000 to welcome Serbia and Montenegro back into the OSCE. The new government had expressed its willingness to host an OSCE mission. The OSCE Mission to the Federal Republic of Yugoslavia was created by the PC in January 2001. The name was changed to the OSCE Mission to Serbia and Montenegro in February 2003, following the state's renaming the month before. More recently, in June 2006 the OSCE mission to Serbia and Montenegro ended and instead two new missions were created: the OSCE Mission to Serbia and the OSCE Mission to Montenegro. This reorganization came about after Montenegro voted to become independent the same month. Thus, Montenegro became the 56th participating-state of the OSCE.

From 2001 onwards, the missions' mandates have remained virtually the same. There are two core tasks: democracy building and managing ethnic tensions. The mission has addressed several areas of democratic governance including elections, the media and local administration. In this regard, the OSCE mission has established a police training center in Mitrovo Polje. The mission has also focused on the status of the

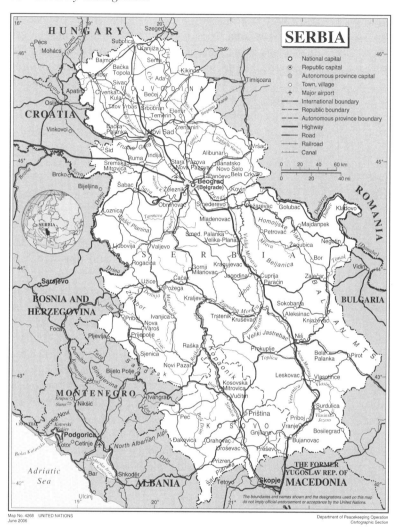

Map 4.6 Serbia.

Source: UN Cartographic Section, No. 4268 June 2006.

significant number of displaced persons produced during the Yugoslav crisis. A considerable number of migrants are Kosovo Serbs who fled during the NATO bombing, were forced out by the KLA or simply were too afraid to remain. Finally, our last case study illustrates well the myriad of OSCE institutions and international organizations working in the region.[55] Within the OSCE, invested actors are the CiO, the CPC, the ODIHR, the HCNM, and the FOM. Among the many organizations and programs involved, the OSCE is working with the European Commission, UN, the Stability Pact for South Eastern, and the Council of Europe as well as a plethora of NGOs including the International Committee of the Red Cross. While there is still a great deal to do, Serbia looks as though it is headed towards peace and stability and the OSCE is one of many organizations there to ensure that it remains on course.

Security management amid burden-sharing

As discussed in Chapter 1, Europe is organizationally well equipped. The post-Cold War era created a series of organizations to deal with security management in addition to the OSCE, including the EU, NATO, and the Western European Union (WEU, much of which has been subsumed into the EU's European Security and Defence Policy), not to mention the UN. How would these organizations be able to work together in order to help manage security and build peace in Europe's areas of conflict? The impediments to cooperation exist on two levels: organizational and state. Organizationally, each of the organizations was trying to stake out a role in the post-Cold War era. The conflicts in Yugoslavia gave the organizations a chance to do just that. However, each of these organizations has its own agenda as well as its own strategies for dealing with conflict situations. The conflicts in Yugoslavia became a testing ground to see what these organizations could do, faced with real conflicts.

Furthermore, individual states had their own agendas in how to treat the conflicts in the Balkans. There were generally three camps in the Euro-Atlantic area. Following the end of the Cold War, many US policy-makers saw a chance to withdraw America's attention away from Europe, since the Soviet threat no longer existed, although this policy would change as the conflicts in Yugoslavia became worse. The US position accorded well within the second camp, the majority of Western European states, who wanted to "Europeanize" the region's mechanisms for security management. Finally, the Russian Federation had its own agenda in the Balkans. Moscow was a traditional supporter of the Yugoslav regime and many Russians sympathized with the Serbian perception that the West was colluding with local ethnic groups to dismantle Yugoslavia. The Yugoslav conflict led Russian relations with the West to deteriorate as the use of force against Serb forces intensified. For example, Russia withdrew from the NATO-Russian

Federation Council upon the initiation of NATO bombing over Kosovo in 1999. Because all the organizations mentioned are intergovernmental organizations, states will attempt to use the organizations that suit their own agendas.

Thus, we see a plethora of organizations becoming involved in managing security and building peace in the Balkans. The US position is constrained because it is not a member of the EU or the WEU. Once the US administration became involved in Bosnia in 1993 and Kosovo in 1999, it relied on the UN and NATO, two organizations of which the United States is a member. Likewise, the European states attempted to work through "European" organizations such as the EU and WEU. No doubt as a response to the Balkans conflicts, the EU has improved its security and defense policies, mostly by subsuming the deployment functions of the WEU. Finally, while Russia is a member of the UN, it is not a member of NATO, the EU, or WEU. Thus, aside from its own foreign policies, Russia relied on the intervention of the OSCE in the region. These competing perspectives among states meant that the countries in the Euro-Atlantic area brought together a plethora of organizations to deal with the Balkan conflicts.

Given the competition between organizations and the interests of the three camps, how is it that the organizations were able to work together? To a large degree, many states are members or participating-states of all of the organizations mentioned. Thus, we can only push the term "competition" so far since the organizations discussed are intergovernmental organizations. Second, the organizations involved did not have contradicting interests or strategies to deal with the conflict. For the OSCE, the EU, NATO, the WEU, and the UN, the point was to prevent any further violence and to rebuild a society that would preclude any future violence. Therefore, in the Balkans, as we shall see more in the next chapter, the organizations were able to use their own particular strategies to resolve the conflict. NATO was employed to bring about an end to violence in Bosnia and later Kosovo. NATO and the EU, along with the WEU, have employed peacekeepers in the region. The UN has concentrated on overseeing peace-building, such as in the guise of the UNMIK. Finally, the OSCE was able to work through its field operations to improve intercommunal dialogue, state–society relations, confidence, and security in the region. Overall, the Balkans conflict has greatly improved the cooperation between the region's organizations and the OSCE, as we will see in Chapter 6.

Conclusion

The norms to support security were established with the Helsinki Final Act and have been further refined over the years. The mechanisms to manage security, however, did not come about until the end of the Cold War. Both the Stockholm Council and Helsinki Summit in 1992 created the core mechanisms that the OSCE uses to manage security. The Stockholm Council established the mandate to initiate OSCE missions. The Helsinki Summit took the steps to refine ODIHR and create a new HCNM. The core objective of the OSCE since has been to support CSBMs in the OSCE region. Our six case studies illustrate both the nature of the OSCE in terms of how it deals with insecurities and also how complex the conflicts in the former Soviet Union and Yugoslavia have been. In terms of the Nagorno-Karabakh conflict, the OSCE has played a constructive role in bringing about initial peace through the Minsk process. For South Ossetia, the OSCE has played the role of third-party actor despite the volatility in Georgian politics and relations with Moscow. The Transdniestrian crisis has left the OSCE few options in the breakaway region itself, although conditions in the remainder of Moldova are improving. Nevertheless, these three conflicts remain frozen and there is little that the OSCE can do to bring about a resolution without the change in position of the Russian Federation. The crisis in the former Yugoslavia is far different although there are still considerable challenges, not to mention that the status of Kosovo is still being debated. These states also have the opportunity to capitalize on the carrots offered by the EU, a road to resolution that the "frozen" conflicts do not have. Having never established a peace-keeping force, the role of the OSCE in these (post-)conflict areas has been primarily to focus on managing nation-building while supporting the establishment of a viable state. The following chapter illustrates another dimension of the OSCE: the human dimension. As we shall see, the focus on democratization and human rights is no less about security and cooperation than the mechanisms of security management discussed in this chapter.

5 Democratization and human rights

Basket III of the OSCE is the "human dimension." The efforts of the framers of the Helsinki Final Act recognized the impact of the human dimension on larger security concerns, not to mention its application to cooperation. As discussed in Chapter 2, there were several groups of actors in the negotiations from 1973 to 1975. The myriad of actors, many of whom were undemocratic states to begin with, relegated Basket III to cultural and information exchange alone. The human dimension, as expressed in the Final Act is limited to two chapters: "human contacts" and "co-operation and exchanges in the field of culture." The discourse of "democracy" and "human rights" had been heavily tainted by the Cold War, making a comprehensive view of the human dimension unattainable at the time the Final Act was created.[1] However, the times and the organization have changed. Beginning in the late 1980s, the CSCE began to expand on the human dimension. The wave of democratization had already begun with the changes in Portugal, Spain, and Greece and the contagion of democratization was spreading eastward.[2] Expanding the human dimension was not only part of supporting democratization and human rights in the Euro-Atlantic area, but was also about preventing ethnic conflict, which had already been witnessed in Yugoslavia and the Soviet Union, as discussed in the previous chapter. Nonetheless, the nature of the CSCE changed with the expansion of the human dimension into the areas of democratization and human rights. This expansion, in turn, had an impact on the organization's ability to cope with human and societal insecurities. This chapter focuses on the OSCE's focus on democratization and human rights in the OSCE area.

The chapter is divided into four sections. First, we take a closer look at the expanding meaning of the human dimension in the OSCE and in particular look at its relationship to democratization and human rights. Second, we discuss the institutions that focus on the human dimension in the OSCE. The chapter focuses on the actions of ODIHR, the HCNM, and the FOM in the OSCE region. Third, we look at the OSCE's overlapping relationship with other international organizations such as the EU and the Council of Europe. Particular attention is given to the cooperation and competition between the organizations. Finally, considerable attention is given to the role of the OSCE in promoting democracy and the protection of human and minority rights in the former Soviet Union and Yugoslavia. Again, six case studies, three from the former Soviet Union, two from the former Yugoslavia, and one former socialist state are included to illustrate the country-level operations of the OSCE and its support for democratization and human rights.

The human dimension

The Belgian CiO has stated that "the OSCE's uniqueness essentially resides in the fact that it is fundamentally concerned with security and stability with an overarching respect for democracy, the rule of law, human rights, and freedoms."[3] Originally, the human dimension was only vaguely linked to human rights, although the United States and its allies viewed the agreement differently than the Soviet Union and its allies.[4] In 1977, for the first follow-up conference in Belgrade following the Final Act, the human rights issue was brought up again but participating states came away without any agreement on the issue.[5] It was perceived that not only had the West submitted too much in the Final Act, but they had not even stood up to the Soviets when it came time to support the progress that had been made in Helsinki.[6] Nevertheless, the nature of the CSCE as being initially an organization for gathering information to support security and cooperation meant that the procedures for examination established by the Final Act would keep human rights on the agenda at subsequent meetings. Unfortunately for the dictatorships in Southern, Central, and Eastern Europe, Portugal's democratic transition in 1974 began what has been referred to as the "third wave" of democratization.[7] By 1985, the Soviet leadership had produced a leader that would transform the Soviet Union. With *glasnost*, Gorbachev began to invigorate Soviet civil society. What followed was the collapse of the socialist regimes throughout Central and Eastern Europe. The political discourse surrounding human rights in the Euro-Atlantic area had changed from that of the Cold War contest between East and West.

Even before the fall of the socialist regimes in Central and Eastern Europe, the CSCE was already working towards expanding the scope of the human dimension. The Third CSCE Follow-up Meeting (the others being in Belgrade and Madrid) took place in Vienna from November 1986 to January 1989. The political face of Central and Eastern Europe changed dramatically during this period. At the end of the meeting, the participating states agreed on a Final Document which calls for the respect of human rights. Vienna was the official beginning of the "human dimension" in the CSCE. Based on the decisions of the Third Follow-up Meeting, the First Meeting of the Conference on the Human Dimension of the CSCE was held in Paris in May 1989. Paris was the first of three meetings to be held on the human dimension The Second Meeting was held in Copenhagen in June 1990. The point of the second meeting was to see how the CSCE was coping with the changes in Europe. The Document of the Second Meeting states:

> The participating States express their conviction that full respect for human rights and fundamental freedoms and the development of societies based on pluralistic democracy and the rule of law are prerequisites for progress in setting up the lasting order of peace, security, justice, and cooperation that they seek to establish in Europe. They therefore reaffirm their commitment to implement fully all provisions of the Final Act and of the other CSCE documents relating to the human dimension and undertake to build on the progress they have made.

As far as this chapter is concerned, we only need to highlight two aspects of this quote. First, we should note the inclusion of "full respect for human rights" as well as "development of societies based on pluralistic democracy." Here, the CSCE was moving beyond the "human contact" and "cultural exchange" notion of a human dimension to include democratization and human rights. Second, we should note the direct link between democracy and human rights as "prerequisites for progress in setting up the lasting order of peace, security, justice, and co-operation that they seek to establish in Europe." This is an explicit link between liberal democracy and peace. Such a link is predicated on the democratic peace theory, e.g. democratic states do not fight other democratic states. The democratic peace is not only an assumption of the OSCE but also many of its participating states. However, Edward Mansfield and Jack Snyder have argued that while stable, liberal democracies may fit well within the democratic peace theory, the road to democracy can be treacherous.[8] They have particularly focused on the conflicts in the former Yugoslavia to illustrate that liberalization does not always create democratization so easily.

The Third Meeting of the Conference on the Human Dimension of the CSCE fittingly took place in Moscow in September and October 1991, shortly before the dissolution of the Soviet Union. The final meeting had special significance as it followed the Paris Charter for a New Europe. Fundamentally, the Moscow meeting is where the participating states took the step to declare that the human dimension mechanisms created in Paris in 1990 were essential parts of the CSCE process. Furthermore, the Moscow meeting set out the procedure for short-term field missions, establishing a process that would allow a mission of experts on the human dimension to enter a state on the request of the participating state. The missions were relatively small compared to the current OSCE missions, with only three individuals. Furthermore, should the state not wish to host a mission of experts, the Moscow Mechanism would allow the CSCE to send a team of rapporteurs. With the Moscow meeting, the consensual role of the participating states in expanding the human dimension for the most part came to an end. Following this, institutions within the organization became both norm-makers and policy implementers.[9] This change was just as well as the CSCE was already learning that consensus would be harder to find.

The OSCE notion of the human dimension has continued to expand. Today, the OSCE covers ten areas under the heading "human dimension." The most routine are education, democratization, human rights, the rule of law, and elections. Freedom of the media came about later with the creation of the FOM in 1997. Minority rights, tolerance, and non-discrimination have also become focal points of the OSCE. Most recently, gender equality and anti-trafficking have also become important parts of the human dimension. OSCE field missions and offices are ordinarily engaged with all of these activities where they apply. The missions are just one institution within the OSCE that deals with the implementation of the human dimension. As discussed in Chapter 3, the OSCE has other institutions that are key norm-setters within the organization as well as the larger international community.

Institutionalizing the human dimension

Since the 1989 Vienna Document laying out the human dimension as indivisibly applying to all participating states as well as linking it to causes of traditional forms of conflict and insecurity, the OSCE has moved to institutionalize the human dimension within the organization. This institutionalization illustrates the transition from conference to organization in that it transfers the responsibility of reports and complaints from participating states (a multi-lateral affair) to the various institutions dealing with the human dimension in the OSCE. This is not to say that participating states do not have an impact on the human dimension, which they maintain through the PC, the CiO, the Parliamentary Assembly, and the secondment of positions, but rather the key mechanisms to deal with routine information gathering, reporting, implementation, and more fundamentally, norm-setting, are held by the OSCE institutions. Every institution in the OSCE addresses the human dimension in some way, although some more than others. We can identify three institutions in the OSCE that have an explicit focus on the human dimension. They are ODIHR, the HCNM, and the FOM. Although we discussed these institutions in Chapter 3, let us see how these institutions relate specifically to the human dimension.

The first institution to be created to deal with the human dimension was the forerunner to ODIHR, the Office for Free Elections. ODIHR has evolved to take on a much larger role in designing and implementing the human dimension. The institution is perhaps best known for election observation, although it is not the only institution to handle this task (i.e. the OSCE Parliamentary Assembly). However, its remit covers nearly the entire gamut of areas associated with the human dimension (combating human trafficking, minority protection, and freedom of the media in particular). In these areas, ODIHR is the key norm-setter within the OSCE. For instance, ODIHR organizes routine meetings concerning the human dimension and its implementation. However, ODIHR's contribution to the human dimension lies with its use of experts and contribution to OSCE missions. Through the use of experts, ODIHR can provide practical support to areas where democratic institutions and human rights require external support. It is also through its own expertise that it is able to help states and other actors deal with outstanding issues related to the human dimension. For example, ODIHR is closely linked to NGOs, especially in the former Soviet Union and has been an important actor behind the "color" revolutions in the region.[10]

ODIHR's ability to act has improved over time. Randolf Oberschmidt describes the sometimes ineffective nature of the institution.[11] He argues that early attempts of the OSCE in general and ODIHR particularly were ineffectual because they lacked focus, operational depth, and remained remote from the area of concern.[12] Capacity was also held back by a culture of minimalism in the organization. In particular, ODIHR had an acute lack of personnel to do the job.

Following the PC's decision to reformulate ODIHR, the institution was able to restructure to become a more effective unit within the OSCE. Capacity for action has improved in ODIHR and its relations with OSCE field activities are key to this change. Oberschmidt argues that ODIHR is more likely to have an impact in (1) missions that have a wider mandate than simply conflict prevention or rehabilitation; and (2) smaller missions.[13] The missions in Georgia and formerly Estonia were primarily focused on preventing conflict and building confidence. While the human dimension was a part of missions, they were better suited towards other institutions, the latter mission dealing with the HCNM. Smaller missions are generally oriented towards the human dimension, such as those formally in Ukraine and Belarus. Where this is the case, the missions are directed and funded by ODIHR. The current debate revolves around ODIHR's ability to disrupt the status quo in the former Soviet Union. Many former Soviet states are unhappy about the OSCE's support for NGOs and grassroots democracy projects in their states. Nevertheless, the actions of ODIHR fit in line with the Vienna Document, the Charter for a New Europe, the Moscow Document, the Copenhagen Document, and nearly every other document pertaining to the human dimension. Let us remember that these documents were based on consensual decisions agreed to by all participating states.

The High Commissioner is perhaps the institution that best illustrates the link between the human dimension and the larger framework for security in the OSCE region.[14] As discussed in Chapter 3, the mandate of the HCNM is to prevent conflict that could result from state–minority relations through the use of "quiet diplomacy."[15] Also as discussed earlier, the notion of "national minorities" is hard to pin down because it lacks a definition in international and European law. Thus, what makes a minority a "national minority" and not an immigrant, asylum seeker, or refugee, assuming that in some cases numbers may be similar, such as in the case of North Africans in France? This dilemma involving the legal definition of a national minority is unnecessary in regards to a political, rather than legal, organization. The High Commissioner and related participating states are making a political decision to term, for example, the Russians in Estonia and Latvia as national minorities while avoiding altogether the issue of Catalans in Spain, the Welsh in the UK, or perhaps most controversially, the Turks in Germany. It is a political decision and a biased decision, but we need to keep in mind that the fundamental task of the HCNM is conflict prevention. Thus, the OSCE has primarily focused on ethnic and/or linguistic minorities that have experienced a change in borders, which points to the states most affected by the legacies of the two world wars and socialism.

The HCNM also works through OSCE field activities, although neither necessarily has a specific mandate to work with the other. One example of where the mission was mandated to work with the HCNM was the OSCE Mission to Estonia that lasted from 1993 to the end of 2001.[16] Ordinarily, however, the High Commissioner works with missions where there is some objective overlap. For example, the way that a state treats its minorities is a reflection of its democratic credentials as much as are free elections. Thus, minorities, democracy, and human rights are closely linked in states where there are defining social cleavages. Otherwise, the HCNM presence in the field is often as a diplomat, observer, and educator. Where there is perceived to be a potential flashpoint, the High Commissioner seeks diplomatic talks with the respective government and the minority community. As observer, the HCNM can turn to the larger OSCE to seek further measures of conflict prevention. Finally, the High Commissioner may act as a promoter of international and European norms surrounding national minorities. Many of the conflicts that were presented in the previous chapter began before the HCNM was established and thus its capacity and effectiveness have not been truly shown in this text. However, there have been considerable success stories in Latvia, Ukraine, Estonia, Bulgaria, Romania, and Slovakia to name only a few.

More recently, the human dimension has been institutionalized in the form of the FOM. Since its inception in 1997, the FOM has focused on freedom of the media across the OSCE region. The FOM is perhaps less geographically biased than ODIHR or the HCNM, where it has reported on journalistic problems in all participating states.[17] The FOM has also recently issued advice on the "Danish cartoons" crisis. Nevertheless, the bulk of the work that the FOM has lies on the areas "East of Vienna." In its work in the field, the FOM works with other OSCE institutions such as ODIHR and the HCNM as well as field missions where the mandate allows and it is thought necessary, such as it has done in Kosovo. The perspective of the FOM is important in this regard. The tasks of the FOM are policy oriented but also focus on the protection of journalists. Importantly, the FOM has maintained that rights *and* responsibilities are part of the overall media package. This perspective is particularly important bearing in mind the security prevention aspects of the larger organization. Overall, the FOM work in the field is an important feature of the OSCE focus on the human dimension. Altogether, the three institutions present the OSCE approach to the human dimension.

The OSCE and the human dimension in context

As stated in the previous chapter, it is often difficult to distinguish between the politico-military aspects of the OSCE and those of the human dimension. However, the OSCE focus on democracy and human rights is primarily part of a conflict prevention mechanism or part of a peace-building strategy. In the previous chapter, other than in the case of Kosovo, many of the conflicts began before the OSCE had a proper response to the crises. Yet, with the focus on the human dimension, there has been considerable progress in these conflicts and other challenges. Again, we use case studies in the former Soviet Union and Yugoslavia as well as one former socialist state to illustrate the OSCE's human dimension in context. In the former Soviet Union, we look at the cases of Latvia, Ukraine, and Kyrgyzstan, a selection that provides a wide range of outcomes. Within the former Yugoslavia, we rely on the cases of Bosnia-Herzegovina and Macedonia. Our final case study is the OSCE presence in Albania. Let us begin with the only EU member-state among our case studies.

Latvia

When the Soviet Union collapsed, 25 million Russians lived outside Russia.[18] Like Estonia, Ukraine, Kazakhstan, Moldova, and other former Soviet republics, Latvia had its share of Russians following independence in August 1991. Before the Second World War, Latvia was an independent state but was "dealt" to the Soviet Union in the power game known as the Molotov–Ribbentrop Pact. Thus, from 1941 onwards, the Soviet Union waged a campaign to subdue Latvia and its other two Baltic neighbors, Estonia and Lithuania. When the Soviets included Latvia in the Union, the republic was one of the most developed and was geo-strategically well placed in the west on the Baltic Sea (Map 5.1). The Soviets used a policy of migration to support the further industrialization, Sovietization, and de-nationalization of Latvia. Anatol Lievan suggests that the intention of the Soviet regime was to dilute the Baltic population as a means of bolstering pro-Soviet loyalties.[19] For the most part, immigrants were industrial workers and technical personnel destined to move on once their jobs were completed. For instance, Ilga Apine estimates that nearly four million people passed through Latvia during the Soviet period, of which 700,000 remained in 1991.[20] By the end of the Soviet era, the non-Latvian population in Latvia had grown from near 10 percent in the interwar period to 48 percent. Latvians were close to becoming minorities in Latvia.

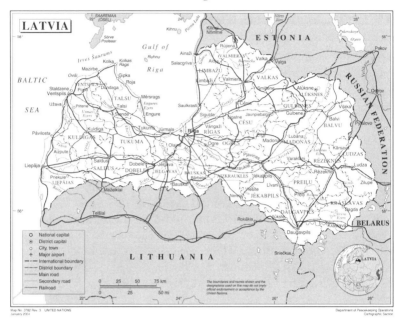

Map 5.1 Latvia.

Source: UN Cartographic Section, No. 3782 Rev. 3 January 2004.

Latvia's independence left a large Russian-speaking[21] minority community. The Latvian political scene following independence was dominated by competing Latvian nationalist parties.[22] Following the 1993 elections, the Latvian parliament passed a citizenship law (1994) that relegated the overwhelming majority of non-Latvians to stateless-ness. The law stated that only citizens and their descendants of the inter-war regime could become automatic citizens. Furthermore, the law established difficult measures for becoming a Latvian citizen.[23] The first was a civic and Latvian language exam that must be passed to gain citizenship. The second was the "windows" system of naturaliza-tion.[24] The system allowed for non-citizens with different statuses to becoming naturalized at different stages. For instance, non-citizen spouses to Latvian citizens could apply in the first "window," while those who had no such connection would be required to wait until 2001, regardless of whether they could pass the examination require-ments. Not only did the 1994 citizenship law leave Latvia with a large stateless community, consisting predominantly of Russians with an at times unstable and rhetorically bellicose Russian Federation as neighbor, but it also meant the great majority of minorities were alienated from the political institutions of Latvia by being refused the right to vote in national or local elections or hold state jobs.

Furthermore, the Latvian government maintained a policy of re-nationalizing the country.[25] For instance, despite the fact that Russians are the largest ethnic group in the capital Riga, nearly the only place to find Cyrillic is on the Russian drama theatre in the Old Town. This re-Latvianization had been carried out in language and education policies. In 1989, the Latvian Supreme Soviet relegated Russian from its official position and promoted Latvian to the sole language of the Latvian SSR. Subsequent language laws have confirmed this position for the titular language. Finally, the Latvian government began in 2004 on a campaign to change school education for minorities from nearly completely in the minority language to slightly over half Latvian and the remainder in the minority language.[26] When Latvia began a new nation-building project following the restitution of independence in 1991, the international community had every reason to think that it could explode into violence as happened in Moldova. Thus, as one of the first organizations that Latvia joined in 1991, the OSCE took a keen interest in national minorities.

OSCE interest in Latvia was focused around the High Commissioner and the OSCE Mission to Latvia.[27] Latvia joined the OSCE quickly after independence. The High Commissioner made his first visit to Latvia in April 1993. At the time, events in Estonia appeared more threatening than they did in Latvia, following the government's approval of a similarly restrictive citizenship law in 1992 and a Law on Aliens in 1993 that established a new procedure to register stateless persons. The High Commissioner visited all three Baltic States and commented on their ethnic relations. Particular attention was drawn to Estonia and Latvia in the resulting HCNM letters to the Baltic governments.[28] The letter to Latvia noted that 93 percent of non-Latvians had lived in Latvia for more than 16 years. Thus, it was unlikely that there would be a mass exodus of Russians to the Russian Federation, regardless of policies. He also suggested the creation of an office of National Commissioner on Ethnic and Language Questions. Such an office was not established until the late 1990s to promote a belatedly established social integration project. Finally, he prompted the Latvian government to develop a constructive citizenship policy that would aim at integrating the large stateless population. After nationalist parties attempted to establish annual quotas in the naturalization process, the High Commissioner stressed a middle way, between exclusion and inclusion: the "windows" system. Eventually, the citizenship law was approved with the segmented system. The High Commissioner returned to Latvia again in 1998 when the Latvian Parliament was reconsidering the law. Van der Stoel took the opportunity to encourage lawmakers to change the citizenship law to except children born since the Soviet period and to abolish the "windows" system. Despite considerable political wrangling, the HCNM program was eventually approved.

The OSCE Mission to Latvia was sent to address the citizenship issue as well as to be at the disposal of the Latvian government for expert advice on democracy and human rights. While the Estonian mission's mandate required that it work with the HCNM, the Latvian mission had no such requirement. The difference in mandates illustrates the perceived threat to security presented by the ethnic situation in Estonia. The OSCE Mission to Latvia did have the ability to cooperate with the High Commissioner as well as other OSCE institutions, such as ODIHR. The mission focused on policy implementation rather than policy-making as the HCNM had done. In particular, the missions established programs to publicize the citizenship requirements and to promote Latvian language learning among the minority communities. The mission also observed the naturalization process to ensure that the law was being implemented fairly. Finally, the OSCE mission supported NGOs in Latvia that concentrated on democratization as well as human and minority rights. In particular, the OSCE was a supporter of the initiatives of the philanthropist George Soros to help build democratically consolidated states. Citing that Latvia had met its requirement, the OSCE Presence was closed, or rather not extended, in December 2001. Today, the OSCE's Presence is similar to that in other Central and Eastern European states that have joined the EU: occasional observations by the HCNM and election observation by ODIHR.

Ukraine

Ukrainian independence in 1991 also brought with it a large Russian community who predominantly live in the East.[29] Ukrainian nationalism and Russian reactive nationalism are more complex than in Latvia.[30] First and foremost, Ukraine is far larger in geographical size and population. There is little doubt that the "small state" status of Latvia and the other Baltic States has had an impact on the potential for violence, albeit size does not always matter as the case of Moldova illustrates. Second, the relationship between Ukrainian and Russian identity is complex. For example, Kievan Rus is the birthplace of both the Ukrainian and Russian nations. Kiev is the capital of Ukraine

(Map 5.2). Furthermore, there has been a close historical link between the Ukrainians and the Russian state, being part of the Russian empire for centuries. This link also has a linguistic dimension. Like Russian, Ukrainian is also an East Slavic language and there are a plethora of shared words. The Ukrainian ethno-political situation is made more complex by a third group: the Crimean Tatars. During the Stalinist period, the Soviet government deported nearly the entire population of Crimean Tatars to Siberia and Central Asia. Once they had been removed, the Crimean Autonomous Soviet Socialist Republic was abolished. Ukrainian independence meant a return of thousands of Crimean Tatars to their national homeland. Overall, the dimensions of inter-ethnic relations as well as state–minority relations are made more difficult where there is a competition between national identities with numerous shared characteristics.

Managing ethnic relations in a democratic state is difficult enough, but when a state is stalling in its transition from authoritarianism to democracy, the situation is much more precarious. Ukrainian politics have been dominated by strong men in strong positions. While the

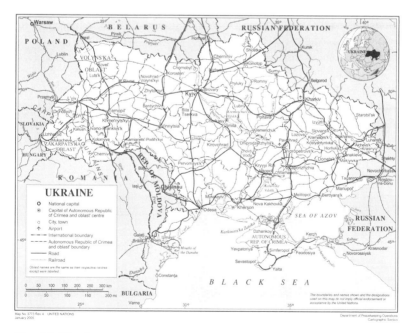

Map 5.2 Ukraine.

Source: UN Cartographic Section, No. 3773 Rev. 4 January 2005.

executive has remained particularly strong, the judicial branch has remained weak. Party politics has been fractious and often unrepresentative. Nevertheless, it is not necessarily the system that is the problem. The 1996 constitution established a political system that represents, on paper, Western democracies (i.e. separation of powers, the rule of law, human rights, and democratic institutions). Yet, the system has not worked. Politics is dominated by economic elites, many of them part of the former Soviet nomenklatura who impede political and economic transition. Until recently, civil society has been unable to affect politics and the media fails to play a strong role in providing a check on politics. Thus, the OSCE has had two primary concerns in Ukraine: minorities and democracy.

The HCNM's first visit to Ukraine was in May 1994. Crimea was a focal point for two reasons.[31] First, the Crimean peninsula was primarily populated by minority Russians who were seeking greater self-determination. In addition, thousands of Crimean Tatars were returning to their national homeland following years of exile under the Soviets. Second, the question that surrounded Crimea is whether it would seek internal or external self-determination. In other words, would the authorities in Simferopol settle for greater autonomy within an independent Ukraine, as Tatarstan had done within the Russian Federation, or would they seek independence altogether? From the beginning, the OSCE through the High Commissioner stressed a "status quo" approach. In his first set of recommendations, van der Stoel recommended that any settlement be based on Ukrainian national integrity and autonomy for the region. The HCNM applied particular stress on building economic links between Crimea and the rest of Ukraine. The High Commissioner's recommendations included a suggestion that a team of constitutional and economic experts be sent to the area to support officials in Kiev and Simferopol.

Seeing a package that they liked, the Ukrainian authorities subsequently requested that an OSCE mission be deployed to Ukraine. The mandate of the mission, established in June 1994, was to support communication between the national government and that of the peninsular as well as to facilitate the aforementioned group of experts.[32] Immediately following the HCNM initial recommendations and the establishment of the OSCE mission to Ukraine, officials in Crimea began to push harder for independence altogether. Kiev responded by requiring the Crimean autonomous constitution be brought in line with the Ukrainian constitution particularly in the area of where power lies. Within a short time, however, both sides agreed to hold talks over the future of Crimea. The Ukrainian position was supported by the OSCE, but the Crimean position was strengthened by Russian interest in Russian minorities in the region and the location of the Russian Black Sea naval base on the peninsula. Yet, there were two further contributors to a peaceful settlement. Crimea experienced a sharp increase in organized crime in the region which shed bad light on the Crimean authorities pushing for autonomy. Second, the pro-Russian Leonid Kuchma won the June 1994 presidential elections. Kuchma was strongly supported in the elections in Crimea. With an impetus for peace, the HCNM and the mission had a constructive situation in which to bring a resolution.

Following the Ukrainian elections, the HCNM and mission were reacting in two different ways. A trademark of the High Commissioner, van der Stoel used "quiet diplomacy" to encourage officials in Kiev and Simferopol to maintain communication. The mission, on the other hand, openly expressed concern over the actions of the Kuchma government who made a unilateral decision to suspend the autonomous powers of Crimea. Other than the mission, the OSCE did not openly condemn the actions of the Ukrainian officials, illustrating once again the "status quo" approach to the disagreement. In May 1995, a round table was established in Locarno, Switzerland to make recommendations on bringing Kiev and Simferopol closer together.[33] Van der Stoel used the opportunity to arrange a meeting of the OSCE team of experts. The Locarno recommendations began a slow process of rapprochement that took several years and several additional meetings arranged by the OSCE. The OSCE mission to Ukraine was closed in April 1999. Eventually, the potential for conflict and instability involving Ukraine and most probably Russia was avoided with the help of the very institutions that the OSCE had created to prevent such confrontations coming to a head. The fact that the OSCE had a chance in which to act following the creation of the HCNM and the missions lends evidence to suggest that other earlier conflicts that remain "frozen" could have benefited from the early warning and mediation that the OSCE now provides from the outset.

Kyrgyzstan

Another former Soviet republic, Kyrgyzstan has come under the focus of OSCE activities more recently than those missions discussed before. Located in a geo-strategically challenging location between China, Kazakhstan, Uzbekistan, and Tajikistan (Map 5.3), Kyrgyzstan has remained relatively stable despite lying in an otherwise unstable area. For instance, Kyrgyzstan lies just north of Afghanistan and Tajikistan

has seen its share of conflict within and with Uzbekistan. Gaining
independence for the first time in 1991 following the dissolution of the
Soviet Union, Kyrgyzstan has been one of many countries that have
failed to transition to a democratic, market economic state. Considerable
challenges exist with human rights abuses, a lack of democratic institutions, abuses against journalists and publishers as well as with ethnic
minorities. More recently, the Kyrgyz authorities allowed NATO
aircraft to use airbases for raids into Afghanistan. However, since the
failed "White Revolution" in 2005, the progress of political and
economic change and Kyrgyz-US relations have become sour.

Fortunately, Kyrgyzstan lacks many of the features that have involved
the OSCE in many places. There is no open or "frozen" conflict between
ethnic groups, regional groups or between Kyrgyzstan and another state.
Unfortunately, as described, the political momentum that came after
independence from the Soviet Union did not lead to a democratic state
or a market economy. Realizing that the organization had something
to provide the state, both the OSCE and Kyrgyzstan decided that a
center would be established in 1998. The OSCE Centre in Bishkek has a

Map 5.3 Kyrgyzstan.

Source: UN Cartographic Section, No. 3770 Rev. 6 January 2004.

mandate to support the basic principles of the OSCE in Kyrgyzstan and in the wider region. Thus, the center and the field office in the southern city Osh have politico-military, economic and environmental as well as human dimensions.[34] The first dimension includes democratization, border issues, and early warning conflict prevention. In conjunction with ODIHR, democratization efforts are focused at improving parliamentary system, civil society, and the overall political party system. The OSCE approach to border issues in Kyrgyzstan revolves around questions of migration and citizenship along border areas. Furthermore, the field office in Osh was established to address the water and land usage issues along the border with Uzbekistan. Early warning conflict prevention also is focused on managing state–minority relations, particularly in the border regions. The OSCE mission mandate specifically requests that the mission work in cooperation with the HCNM.

The second dimension surrounds environmental and economic issues in Kyrgyzstan. The OSCE primarily works through education to promote environmental awareness. In the work on the environment, we see legacies of the initial concerns illustrated in the Final Act. For instance, a great deal of concern is focused on trans-boundary environmental crises. In this case, the mission works to ensure the implementation of environmental conventions such as the Conventions on Transboundary Impact Assessment and Trans-boundary Industrial Accidents. The OSCE has also established the Environment and Security Initiative (ENVSEC) in Kyrgyzstan to work on early-warning mechanisms for environmental crises, such as identifying potential landslides. Economically, Kyrgyzstan has many of the problems associated with other developing states around the world, such as low levels of capital, capital flight, corruption, organized crime, and general widespread poverty. The OSCE mission has been working towards developing anti-corruption policies and good-governance initiatives as a means of promoting economic growth. Furthermore, there has been a special focus on small and medium-sized businesses as well as promoting the participation of women in the economy. In order for the economy to grow, there needs to be a viable state in which businesses can work. For this reason, much of the work in Kyrgyzstan has been focused on institution building and organizing commercial interests. The OSCE role in Kyrgyzstan is important especially because unlike many of our other case studies, the OSCE is the only regional organization to lend development support, whereas states in the former Yugoslavia will have support from a plethora of organizations.

Finally, the human dimension is focused on political reform, human rights, and anti-trafficking programs. Political reform includes police reform, changes in prison sentences and introducing other forms of punishment, promoting public participation in political reform, supporting NGOs, and improving the justice system. The focus on human rights includes the support for media development, the introduction of civic textbooks in schools, supporting the Advocacy and Human Rights Center, as well as monitoring detention centers. Anti-trafficking programs include the OSCE working with the government and NGOs to help prevent the trafficking of human beings. A vital part of this is promoting the role of women in the political system and Kyrgyz society in general. Finally, the OSCE mission has established an OSCE Academy in Bishkek to educate locals in areas of comprehensive security. The academy brings these three dimensions together to illustrate the core of the OSCE principles as defined in the Final Act and Charter of Paris.

Bosnia-Herzegovina

As discussed in Chapter 4, Bosnia's independence from Yugoslavia was the hardest won. Also, while many of the other former Yugoslav states are now quite ethnically homogeneous, although none completely, Bosnia remains an ethnically diverse state with a sizable Serbian population in the southeast, contiguous with the Bosnian-Serbian border (Map 5.4). There also remains a Croatian minority in Bosnia but this is less a problem given the Croatian-Bosniak alliance in the latter years of the Bosnian War. Bosnia has had organizational support from the UN, the EU, NATO, and the Council of Europe. In contrast to Kyrgyzstan, the OSCE is just one of many organizations in Bosnia. Nevertheless, the OSCE role in Bosnia has been important for peace-building and state-building in the region. As this chapter focuses on the human dimension, the discussion is tailored towards democratization and human rights in Bosnia. However, for an organization that focuses on comprehensive security, it is impossible to get away from the traditional security measures that are obviously going on in Bosnia. The OSCE was named in the Dayton Peace Accords as one of the main organizations to support Bosnia. From Dayton, the OSCE mission to Bosnia and Herzegovina was created in December 1995.[35]

The OSCE operations in Bosnia have been primarily aimed at the local level as opposed to the national level.[36] Thus, the OSCE mission is broken down into four centers in Banja Luka, Mostar, Sarajevo, and Tuzla, and field offices in 22 municipalities across the entire country. The mission has four focus areas. These are democratization, education, human rights, and security cooperation. Each of the four focus

Map 5.4 Bosnia-Herzegovina.

Source: UN Cartographic Section, No. 3729 Rev. 5 June 2004

areas has its own director. For our purposes, we will look at the first three. The democratization department supports the parliamentary system, local government, civic engagement with politics, and civil society. The parliamentary support project has focused on parliamentary oversight as well as establishing a press gallery. The mission has supported local governance in terms of finance and human resources management. The OSCE has also supported public engagement with local government as well as supported best-practices programs through an exchange system. Civic engagement is supported in the innovative UGOVOR program launched in March 2005. The program focuses on five areas:

1   Freedom of access to public information.
2   Code of ethics for elected officials.
3   Participatory strategic planning.
4   Harmonization of municipal statutes.
5   Municipal-citizen partnership.

UGOVOR is in addition to the local government support project. Finally, the Democratization Department promotes civil society in Bosnia in terms of supporting NGOs to engage with local issues of concern.

The education program was established following the UN High Representative's request that the OSCE take on the education sector. The OSCE supports the education system by encouraging a non-political environment in schools. Through the "Interim Agreement on Accommodation of the Specific Needs and Rights of Returnee Children," the OSCE has helped promote the return of families to their pre-war homes by providing increased numbers of schools for returnees. Furthermore, the OSCE has supported a program on supporting the needs of the Roma and other national minorities in the education system. Finally, the OSCE mission has attempted to increase the civic engagement with the education system. Increasing civic engagement is also about educating parents to get involved with their children's education as well as holding workshops about how parents can impact education policy. The OSCE role in providing for a reformed education system illustrates the continuing presence of the organization even where there is considerable organizational overlap.

The human rights department focuses on several rights-based areas. First, economic and social rights are supported by ensuring that public services are provided to everyone, regardless of ethnicity or disability. The health service is one such public service. Second, the OSCE supports minority rights in Bosnia, at times in conjunction with the HCNM. The focus on minority rights also includes access to education, housing, and other public services. Third, the OSCE mission supports institutional mechanisms within the Bosnian government where human rights violations can be independently treated and resolved. The OSCE has participated with the EU and the Council of

Europe to create a human rights ombudsman in Bosnia. Fourth, the human rights department is focused on preventing the trafficking of human beings by establishing a monitoring mechanism and seeking policy reforms to assist bringing traffickers to justice. Fifth, and in connection, the OSCE supports criminal justice reform through the Criminal Codes Implementation Assessment Team (CCIAT). Finally, the OSCE has been involved with the difficult task of monitoring trials to ensure an independent, unbiased justice system. While Bosnia received the worst end of the fighting in the Yugoslav wars, the state has also received the most support from international organizations. Through these support departments, the OSCE Mission to Bosnia and Herzegovina has helped Bosnia overcome conflict, build peace and a viable state.

FYR Macedonia[37]

The OSCE Spillover Monitor Mission to Skopje is the longest-serving field activity in the organization. Created in 1992, the OSCE saw that the tensions in the former Yugoslav area could possibly spread to Macedonia. The primary issue was the border tensions with the then Yugoslavia (Serbia). More belatedly, Macedonia saw increasing tensions between ethnic Macedonians and ethnic Albanians. Similar to the case in Moldova or Latvia, an independent Macedonia helped promote a nationalist movement that continued into the post-Yugoslav era. In response, many Albanians felt threatened by a "Macedonianization" while others were seeking a greater Albania, as we saw in Kosovo in Chapter 4. The fact that the Skopje mission is the longest-serving OSCE field activity says something about the nature of the challenges in the state in the beginning and the failure of the international community to bring an end to them. The OSCE mission in Macedonia looks similar to many of the other missions, but is specific to the country itself.

The OSCE Spillover Mission to Skopje was the first long-term mission to be established although the CSCE had used short-term rapporteur missions previously. The mission has been through three phases. From 1992 to 1998, the mission mandate was to observe the border between Macedonia and Serbia (Map 5.5). Observers were to monitor a firm border and any incidents which could lead to greater conflict between Macedonia and the Yugoslav forces. Within this mandate, the mission began to extend beyond simply border observation. In particular, the mission was given the tasks of liaising with the host government in Skopje, political parties, and citizens groups. Thus, the OSCE was not only interested in working towards a stable border, but also a stable, viable Macedonia. The phase was from 1998 to 2000. Tensions in Kosovo were growing following the withdrawal of Yugoslav troops from Bosnia. The OSCE was well aware that tensions were growing since it had deployed the OSCE Kosovo Verification Mission. Thus, in March 1998, the OSCE Spillover Mission to Skopje mandate was expanded to cover observation of the border with Serbia and Kosovo. Noting that Kosovo was a part of the same Yugoslavia whose border the mission was set to observe in 1992, the focus in 1998 became specifically the rise in tension between ethnic Macedonians and ethnic Albanians. Finally, since September 2001, the OSCE mission has been tasked with a broad mandate which includes border monitoring, observing the humanitarian situation, the trafficking of human beings, as well as working with refugees and other displaced persons. Above all, the OSCE mission is set to monitor the ceasefire agreement between the Macedonian government and the Albanian forces. The OSCE Spillover Mission to Skopje set the template for subsequent missions in the beginning, but it has also changed as both

Map 5.5 FYR Macedonia.

Source: UN Cartographic Section, No. 3789 Rev. 4 January 2004.

the OSCE and the mission area has changed. As the former Yugoslav area changes from reconciliation to peace- and state-building, so too the mission has changed.

Albania[38]

The OSCE Presence in Albania is one of the latter additions to the list of OSCE field activities, established in 1997. Like so many of our case studies, Albania has its own unique challenges to overcome following its break with socialist authoritarianism (Map 5.6). The state remains one of the poorest regions in Europe and has been guilty of everything from fostering guerrilla movements in neighboring states to being the center of illicit and human trafficking in Europe. The OSCE Presence in Albania is vital for the state to begin some kind of socio-political normalization. The operation began following a breakdown of social order in 1997. Albania's challenges primarily revolved around low levels of state-capacity and the lack of democratic institutions. In this regard, the OSCE Presence in Albanian was established to address three core areas. First, the OSCE mandate was to support democratic institutions, the media and human rights. In this regard, ODIHR and the FOM have been important liaisons. Second, the OSCE Presence has been tasked with election preparation and monitoring. Again, close cooperation between the field presence and ODIHR is important.

Finally, the OSCE mandate includes addressing the consequences of the Kosovo conflict. Thousands of refugees crossed into Albania from Kosovo at first when the Yugoslav forces entered and then when NATO bombing began in 1999. In this regard, the OSCE Presence co-chaired an information donor forum from 1998–2002 during the height of the crisis. The OSCE Presence has also been tasked with monitoring the border between Kosovo and Albania in order to control guerrilla movements and refugee flows. Border monitoring includes police support and assistance that has greater impact on policy actions and law throughout Albania. At the time of writing, the OSCE Presence in Albania has five office locations throughout the country. The OSCE benefits from working with other international organizations such as the Council of Europe in Albania, but also individual participating states that independently devote more attention to the state. In recent years, the focus on anti-trafficking has grown in the OSCE as it has in the Council of Europe. As long as Albania remains at the center of the illicit trade of goods and human beings, Europe needs international involvement in Albania. The OSCE Presence in Albania is a pillar of this involvement.

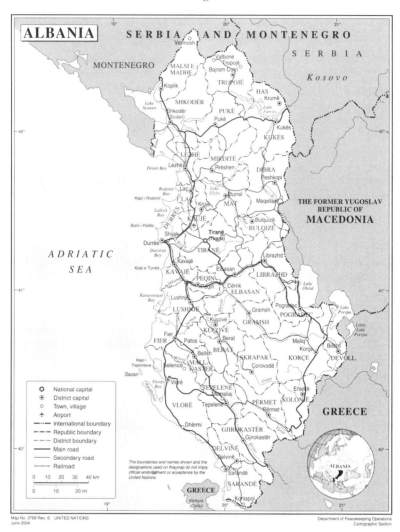

Map 5.6 Albania.

Source: UN Cartographic Section, No. 3769 Rev. 6 June 2004.

Conclusion

The OSCE focus on the human dimension has evolved over time to become what it is today. Cold War politics made discussion of democracy and human rights politically divisive. The Final Act provided for an initial focus on the human dimension, although it focused more on what the Council of Europe was already doing at its most basic level: cultural exchange. Nevertheless, there was enough in the Final Act to allow the West to continue to criticize human rights violations in the Socialist bloc. Within the East itself, Helsinki groups, named after the Final Act, became important players in the socialist regimes. As the Soviet leadership changed, first unwilling to repress Poland and eventually opening political debate in the Soviet Union, the human dimension took on new importance. Europe was in the middle of its "third wave" with the collapse of the socialist regimes and the spread of democracy in Central and Eastern Europe, though at varying paces. However, eventually, the human dimension took on a further importance. As the socialist regimes began to collapse, two failed states erupted in conflict. Societal and human insecurities played important parts in producing conflict in the former Soviet Union and Yugoslavia. The OSCE was already evolving to address these issues, with the Meeting on the Human Dimension, the Charter for a New Europe, and eventually the Copenhagen and Budapest Documents, the OSCE was able to address many of the insecurities in the Euro-Atlantic area. Through strengthening democratic institutions, human rights, and the role of the media in divided states, the OSCE has attempted to make this area a safer place.

6 The OSCE and the European security architecture

The CSCE was born of a certain moment in the Cold War but the OSCE has remained one of the primary regional organizations in post-Cold War Europe. Born out in the Helsinki Final Act, the CSCE approach centered on common and comprehensive security for the Euro-Atlantic community of states. During the Cold War, the CSCE was a step towards decelerating the nuclear contest between the United States and its allies, seen in NATO, and the USSR and its allies, seen in the Warsaw Pact. Furthermore, the Final Act finalized the peace of the Second World War. All borders within the CSCE region were recognized and those who were in power were allowed to remain in power. Above all, the CSCE was an inclusive factor in the Cold War European security architecture. Through recognizing borders and regimes as well as promoting CSBMs in the Euro-Atlantic area, the CSCE became more than a series of conferences but instead a path to preventing conflict between states. However, as the socialist regimes began to crack, the propensity of inter-state conflict lessened and the proclivity for intra-state conflict increased. As early as 1986, the CSCE participating states came together to begin discussing the link between the human dimension and European security as well as what the CSCE could do to promote security and cooperation. This discussion was the beginning of the transition from the "Conference on" to the "Organization for."

The OSCE in the post-Cold War era remains an important part of the European security architecture. In this chapter, we look at the OSCE's evolving role in increasing security and cooperation. What role has the conference and organization played in bringing and keeping peace in the Euro-Atlantic area? In order to answer this question, we have to engage with two summary discussions. First, the chapter brings together the principles and mechanisms of the CSCE/OSCE as a means of seeing the major themes and developments over time. The argument put forward is that overall, the OSCE has been shaped more by its region than the organization has shaped the region. Second, the chapter looks at the collaboration and competition between the OSCE and the other organizations that comprise the European security architecture, such as NATO, the EU, the Council of Europe, and the UN. The second argument is that despite the niche capabilities of the OSCE, the organization is more effective only as it further collaborates with other regional and international organizations. Engaging with these two discussions will allow us to examine the prospects for the future, seen in the following chapter.

Conference and organization

The development of the CSCE and the OSCE has come about with peaks and troughs. Following Soviet foreign policy initiatives to agree to Moscow's projection of power in Central and Eastern Europe in the 1950s and 1960s as well as West Germany's *Ostpolitik* in the late 1960s, the Helsinki process got off to a good start in 1973 with the final culmination being the Final Act in 1975. Within the Final Act, the concentration was on sovereignty, confidence, and security. As now, the CSCE was only one such attempt to bring about stability in Europe, as discussed in Chapter 2. Détente represented a change (if temporary) in the Cold War politics between East and West. Remarkably, born out of the *Zeitgeist* of Détente, the CSCE remained a viable process even after relations between the United States and USSR became sour over the Soviet invasion of Afghanistan and subsequent American incursions in Latin America. Between the Soviet invasion of Afghanistan in 1979 and the promotion of Gorbachev to the head of the Soviet Union in 1985, the CSCE process had little impact on security or cooperation in Europe. Returning to the first argument, as the tension between states rose during this period, the CSCE had little impact on the Euro-Atlantic area but instead represented the condition of participating states. Nevertheless, the legacy of the Final Act still mattered. So-called "Helsinki groups" were challenging repressive regimes across the Socialist bloc. Also, the Soviet authorities were less likely to send troops to quell organized resistance against Socialist regimes as they had done with Hungary in 1956 and Czechoslovakia in 1968. For example, the rise of the Solidarity (*Solidarność*) Movement in Poland in 1980 did not lead to a Warsaw Pact invasion.

Following changes in the Cold War politics after 1985, we see a rise in activity in the CSCE that had not occurred on such a scale since the Helsinki Process. First, the nature of security in Europe was changing and the participating states began to focus more on the third basket, as illustrated in Chapter 5. As early as 1986, the CSCE participating states began discussing the human dimension in the Third Follow-up Meeting in Vienna. At its conclusion in 1989, the CSCE began a series of meetings on the human dimension. Second, the cooperative nature of relations following the fall of the Berlin Wall in 1989 led participating states to sign the CFE Treaty in 1990. While outwith the auspices of the CSCE, the treaty was closely related to the CSBMs promoted by the Helsinki Final Act and included nearly all of the CSCE participating states including all the Warsaw Pact and NATO countries.

As discussed in Chapter 3, the change in the nature of European security led the CSCE to institutionalize its principles into employable mechanisms of security and cooperation in the "new Europe." The Charter of Paris in 1990 set out the original permanent institutions, known today as the Permanent Council, OSCE Secretariat, Parliamentary Assembly, the CPC, and ODIHR. The Helsinki Document in 1992 further broadened the base of institutions with the establishment of the HCNM and the FSC. The Stockholm Summit in December 1992 further elaborated the CSCE's ability to bring peaceful settlements to disputes with the creation of long-term missions, the first being deployed in FYR Macedonia, as discussed in Chapter 5. While the CSCE became an organization with a permanent presence in 1990 and was further developed in 1992, the change from conference to organization did not take place until 1994 at the Budapest Summit. The last of the institutions, the FOM, was established in 1996 at the Lisbon Summit as an extension of the OSCE's focus on the human dimension. However, since 1996, a "deepening" in the OSCE has ended, although new initiatives have been integrated into the OSCE Secretariat, such as human trafficking.

In order to illustrate how the OSCE fits into the European security architecture, let us look at how the organization deals with both security and cooperation in Europe. We have already stated that the OSCE approach to security is "common and comprehensive." By common security, the OSCE is primarily concerned with security within the OSCE area. In recent years the OSCE has had limited operations outside the OSCE region, especially in Afghanistan following the US-led invasion. So-called "out of area" operations are not official OSCE policy, but have occurred based on a specific request by the Kabul government to help in running the 2005 elections. Afghanistan's relationship with the OSCE has developed through the Asian Partners for Co-operation program which it joined in 2002. By comprehensive security, the OSCE approach to security covers all routes to instability, but particularly traditional or strategic security, economic, and environmental security, and human security. While the OSCE remains engaged in the "frozen conflicts," as discussed in Chapter 4, the OSCE has appeared to focus increasingly more on the human dimension. As discussed in Chapter 1, traditional European security is dominated by NATO and its PfP program. In addition, the EU is increasingly taking on a greater role through its ESDP. On the second dimension, the OSCE has few resources to treat economic and environmental security, not to mention that the EU is much better placed in this regard. Overall, "common and comprehensive" security represents the OSCE approach, not to mention contribution, to European security.

To illustrate the OSCE approach further, let us focus on three concepts: state, sovereignty, and conflict prevention. What is the role of the state in the OSCE? Decision-making in the OSCE is based on consensus alone and thus the state retains a great deal of agenda setting in the organization. While it is one state, one vote, some states are more equal than others based on their ability to pull influence in their direction, such as voting on policies in the Permanent Council. The United States and the Russian Federation remain dominant players in the European security architecture and thus also in the OSCE. Unfortunately for both, the two states are often poles apart on events in the post-Soviet region not to mention the further development of the OSCE. In almost all cases, EU member-states vote together and the European Council Presidency speaks on behalf of all EU member-states assuming that an agreement can be reached. With 56 OSCE participating states and 27 EU member-states, the EU's capacity for agenda-setting should be at least on a par with the United States and Russia in the OSCE. However, a participating state has the most agenda-setting power when it holds the CiO position, which lasts for one year, but with a year before and a year after on the "Troika." For example, long-term missions are often the result of a request by the CiO. Recent activities, such as combating terrorism and gender main-streaming, have also been the result of CiO decisions. Nevertheless, the role of the state in the OSCE remains particularly strong given the consensus voting in the PC and at summits. This is illustrated by the deadlock over reform.

What approach does the OSCE have towards national sovereignty in Europe? "Sovereign equality," "inviolability of frontiers," "territorial integrity," and "non-intervention in internal affairs" were all mentioned in the Final Act Decalogue. As discussed in Chapter 2, the reasons behind each of these Helsinki principles are complicated, no less because of the political bargaining that occurred during the Helsinki meetings. Inter-state conflict in the OSCE region has been rare. While the conflicts in the former Yugoslavia could be seen as inter-state, they could also be seen as conflict of state collapse (i.e. Yugoslavia). The conflict in Nagorno-Karabakh can also be seen as inter-state but the Armenians never officially fought against Azerbaijan, although Nagorno-Karabakh Armenians definitely had support from the Armenian military. In the former Soviet Union, the OSCE has tended towards preserving national integrity or sovereignty. The OSCE position on the four "frozen conflicts" is evident. As discussed in Chapters 4 and 5, the OSCE approach in the former Yugoslavia has been similar except in the case of Kosovo. Serbia is intent on Kosovo remaining part of Serbia, albeit with considerable autonomy. There is also a fear in Belgrade that an independent Kosovo will lead to a greater Albania. The Kosovo Albanians have declared their independence, although no-one has recognized the state as independent. However, the OSCE is an active member of the managed separation of Kosovo from Serbia, whether for good or bad. The status of Kosovo is in fact a priority of the 2006 Belgian CiO. The OSCE approach to Kosovo is in stark contrast to the organization's approach to the status of Nagorno-Karabakh, where an equal intransigence exists. The overwhelming difference is the role of the EU in the Balkans as opposed to the lack of organizations in the Nagorno-Karabakh case. Nevertheless, the OSCE approach to Kosovo remains rare in its overall approach to security in the Euro-Atlantic area.

However, the OSCE itself may be one of the prime violators of state sovereignty. In Serbia and Montenegro, in 2000, there was a popular uprising against Miloševic that eventually led to his removal. In Georgia in 2003, another popular uprising known as the Rose Revolution led to the election of a pro-Western, anti-Russian Mikhail Saakashvili as president. The Ukrainian Orange Revolution prevented a pro-Russian presidential candidate from taking office and instead the pro-Western Victor Yushchenko became president. Most recently, Montenegro has become the fifty-sixth participating state of the OSCE following a referendum for independence that only barely passed the threshold for separation. In all of these cases, and others, the OSCE has been an important player in supporting civil society groups who came to challenge these regimes through the work of ODIHR. Now, Russian authorities are wary of ODIHR in its "near abroad." Belarussian authorities have become downright hostile, believing that the OSCE, along with the EU, are intent on removing the Alexander Lukashenko regime. Earlier events suggest that officials in Moscow and Minsk have reason to worry. This skepticism has increasingly made the job of the OSCE more difficult in these regions and has put reform of the organization out of the question for the time being.

Much of what the OSCE does today can be described as conflict prevention, which entails an understanding of comprehensive security. The OSCE approach to conflict prevention is based on the employment of CSBMs.[1] These mechanisms were discussed in the Final Act as a way of preventing conflict in the Euro-Atlantic area within the context of the Cold War. As discussed in Chapters 1 and 2, the CSCE approach to conflict prevention in the Cold War was based on transparency and information. The OSCE approach to conflict prevention is much the same today, although the nature of insecurities has changed with the end of the Cold War. Traditional conflict prevention is best illustrated in the FSC, created in 1990. In the FSC, participating state delegations meet once a week to discuss arms control and CSBMs. The changing nature of conflict means that the HCNM and the CPC are also involved in prevention. The HCNM is first and foremost an institution of conflict prevention, through the employment of information gathering, monitoring, and quiet diplomacy. The CPC coordinates the field missions and other field activities. Together, they have been able to promote CSBMs that concentrate far more on internal, comprehensive security rather than inter-state, common security.

The OSCE remains an important part of the European security architecture and the role of the state, the approach to national sovereignty, and to conflict prevention illustrates this. Nevertheless, the OSCE does not have the resources or often the political will to become the main organization in most of the conflicts in the OSCE area. Partly, the important role of the state in the OSCE makes consensus far more difficult. Yet, at the same time, consensus among often opposing viewpoints is also what makes the OSCE a different organization from other organizations in the European security architecture. As we shall see, the OSCE has a role to play in preventing conflict and building peace and has particular niche capabilities that other organizations do not. But, only in conjunction with these other organizations will the OSCE remain an effective participant in the European security architecture.

Organizational collaboration and competition

What are the OSCE's niche capabilities? Traditionally, the CSCE was good at providing dialogue between opposing parties (i.e. NATO and the Warsaw Pact). Yet, now the OSCE has been accused of being nothing more than a "talking box."[2] If this were the only thing that the OSCE was, it would be problematic, but nevertheless that still would not make the organization irrelevant. The OSCE is the only organization, other than the UN, that consists of North America, Europe, and the entire post-Soviet region. While NATO, the EU, and the Council of Europe have expanded since the end of the Cold War, they are considerably unlikely to go this far. Thus, with every other regional organization, there remain insiders and outsiders. The OSCE's inclusiveness makes it a vital organization for peace and stability in the Euro-Atlantic area, even if it were only a "talking box."

The OSCE also maintains important niche capabilities that are centered on epistemic input, quiet diplomacy, focus on national minorities and its presence in the field. First, the OSCE's epistemic input, or knowledge-base, is an important part of its institutions including the Secretariat, ODIHR, the HCNM, and the FOM. For example, we discussed how both the HCNM and FOM have engaged with academics and practitioners to further develop the principles and norms of minority rights and the freedom of the media. The OSCE epistemic input has been recognized by other organizations such as in the European Commission Regular Reports on enlargement. Second, the OSCE has employed quiet diplomacy as a way of encouraging states and other actors to hold to their commitments under the OSCE and other organizations. As we discussed before, quiet diplomacy is best embodied by the High Commissioner. Max van der Stoel was keen to use public diplomacy on those occasions when it would bring about the most pressure to change. However, after 1998, van der Stoel and his successor Rolf Ekeus have chosen to use quiet diplomacy as a way of bringing opposing parties together. Third, again embodied in the HCNM, the OSCE is the only organization to have a specific institution for dealing with national minorities in terms of conflict prevention. As we shall see, the Council of Europe has not only made use of the HCNM but has also established its own body for dealing with minority rights protection, but less in terms of security and more in terms of democracy. Finally, the OSCE is important in the European security architecture because of its presence in the field with long-term missions and field offices across the former Soviet Union and Yugoslavia. In some cases, the OSCE is the only international presence there. The field activities are important because they facilitate the other mechanisms for security and cooperation in Europe. Furthermore, it is often through the OSCE field activities that other organizations "tap into" certain states. Nevertheless, despite the OSCE epistemic input, quiet diplomacy, focus on national minorities and its presence in the field, the organization is not the paramount security organization in Europe. Returning to our second argument, the OSCE remains important in the European security architecture because it is able to collaborate with other organizations.[3]

When it comes to hard security guarantees in Europe, NATO is the paramount organization, as was seen in the former Yugoslavia. The objectives of the OSCE and NATO have overlapped from the beginning since all the NATO member-states were in fact CSCE participating states. As the CSCE changed into the OSCE, and with all the developments that went with this change, NATO was also going through its own transition, beginning with the 1990 London Declaration. In 1994, NATO began the PfP program which established a strategic relationship with states in the former Socialist bloc, not to mention several neutral states such as Sweden and Ireland. Thus, NATO also became an organization for security and cooperation in Europe. Following the terrorist attacks on 11 September 2001, both NATO and the OSCE changed to focus more on terrorism as a source of instability in the region. In 2004, at the NATO Istanbul Summit, the OSCE Ministerial Council met with NATO member-states and declared that the two organizations had overlapping goals of "conflict prevention, crisis management and post-conflict rehabilitation."[4] The two security organizations have considerable collaboration. The OSCE CiO addresses the North Atlantic Council on a regular basis and the NATO Secretary General addresses the OSCE PC. Also, OSCE observers often participate in NATO-led planning exercises. Perhaps the clearest example of OSCE collaboration has come with the NATO-led KFOR (Kosovo) and SFOR (BiH) missions. In these cases, the two organizations have worked together to implement the Dayton Peace Accords. More recently, NATO forces provided security for OSCE election support teams in Afghanistan.

OSCE–EU relations have been equally cooperative but there has been a considerable amount of competition as well, especially as the EU expands in areas usually associated with the OSCE's human dimension. Cooperation between the two organizations has been ongoing since the Italian European Council Presidency signed the Final Act on behalf of the European Community in 1975. Considering that before 2004, the overwhelming majority of the OSCE participating states were outside the EU, OSCE–EU relations took off in a practical way following the development at Maastricht in 1992 of the Common Foreign and Security Policy (CFSP) and the establishment of the EU enlargement process at Copenhagen in 1993. Since the enlargement in 2004, not to mention forthcoming enlargements, as well as the stabilization and association agreements, the role of the EU in the wider OSCE region has grown. Today, cooperation between the OSCE and EU covers soft security issues such as border management as well as democratization and marketization efforts such as judicial reform and entrepreneurial development. The "framework for cooperation" between the OSCE and EU consists of several contacts. For instance, the OSCE Troika meets with the heads of the European Commission, Council, and Parliament. As discussed, the EU Presidency addresses the OSCE PC during weekly sessions. The European Commission also maintains a delegation in Vienna. Finally, the OSCE and EU often invite representatives of the organization for informal meetings and working groups on common objectives.

Competition between the OSCE and the EU has come about as the latter institution has developed an interest in activities ordinarily associated with the OSCE. An example is election observation. In the Ukrainian elections at the end of 2004, election observers were present from the OSCE, the EU, and the Council of Europe, which begs the question, why were three regional organizations required to do the same job? Perhaps the OSCE's position has been compromised since some of its key participating states, such as the Russian Federation, have heavily criticized the work of ODIHR and the Parliamentary Assembly in monitoring elections in the post-Soviet area. Moscow has charged the OSCE of being regionally biased against the East. The last few years have seen the OSCE monitor elections in Western OSCE participating states, such as the Canadian elections in 2006. Furthermore, the Russian Federation, not liking the work of ODIHR in the post-Soviet region, has taken to submitting election observers of their own, beginning in 2002, in order to balance the Western bias in ODIHR's conclusions.[5] While normally states would be restricted as to how many observers they could send, Russia sent hundreds more than the quota for the Belarussian elections in 2006. Unfortunately for Moscow, the positive observations of the elections did not make it into the final ODIHR conclusions. Furthermore, perhaps the EU can employ a revolutionary foreign policy towards transitioning states more so than can the OSCE. Brussels is only restricted by its own member-states, the majority favoring a constructive engagement for change in states whose transition has stalled. The EU's European Neighborhood Policy seeks a stable and democratic border both in the East and South. In the end, though, as discussed in Chapter 1, two organizations doing the same job means duplication, inefficiency and a waste of resources. Increased collaboration in overlapping areas is vital for the continued relevance of the OSCE.

The overlap with the Council of Europe is similar, but the OSCE's human dimension and the Council of Europe's traditional focus on democracy and human rights are complementary. This liaison between the two organizations can be constructive since the fundamental objectives of the OSCE, security and cooperation, and the Council of Europe, democracy and human rights, are similar but not necessarily competitive. Furthermore, while the OSCE is a political organization, the Council of Europe relies on legal commitments. The OSCE's relationship with the Council of Europe strengthened as the CSCE began to focus more on areas ordinarily associated with the Council of Europe such as democratization and human rights. The CSCE had a comparative advantage simply because it included the transitioning states, which the Council of Europe did not. But, as the countries in Central and Eastern Europe began to seek entrance into the Council of Europe, the CSCE and the Council of Europe were able to focus on similar areas of reform. For example, legislative reform particularly to do with language and citizenship was often a subject of concern for both organizations. The OSCE was concerned that conservative and/or nationalist laws may bring about deterioration in state–minority relations leading to conflict. The Council of Europe's perception of nationalist policies was rooted in concerns over the nature of democratization and fundamental human rights. HCNM country reports on the Baltic States, Bulgaria, and Slovakia offer examples of how the OSCE has relied on and collaborated with the Council of Europe to encourage legislative reform. The relationship between the HCNM and the Council of Europe changed after the Council of Europe initiated the Framework Convention for the Protection of National Minorities in 1995. As a legal treaty, the Framework Convention establishes a level of protection for national minorities in Europe.[6] As more states became both OSCE and Council of Europe participating/member-states, the European Commission often relied on the other two organizations as monitors of accession states preceding the 2004 enlargement, particularly in areas of political reform.[7]

Like the relationship with the EU, the OSCE's relationship with the Council of Europe has become more formal in recent years. In 2000, the two organizations came together when the respective Secretaries General signed a "Common Catalogue of Co-operation Modalities," which established a general structure of institutional contacts. Annual 2+2 meetings occur, consisting of the OSCE CiO and Secretary General with the Council of Europe Chairman of the Committee of Ministers and Secretary General. There are also regular visits by the OSCE CiO and Council of Europe Chairmanship to the other organization's decision-making bodies (the OSCE PC and Council of Europe Committee of Ministers). More recently, the Council of Europe has established a Rapporteur Group on Relations with the OSCE (GR-OSCE). Other institutions within the OSCE have also established formal cooperation with the Council of Europe. ODIHR cooperates often with the Parliamentary Assembly of the Council of Europe as well as the Venice Commission (tasked with legal reform). The HCNM has cooperated with the Council of Europe from its beginning as illustrated earlier and this relationship has continued to grow particularly between the High Commissioner and the Council of Europe Secretariat of the Framework Convention. Often the HCNM relies on both OSCE and Council of Europe treaties and agreements to press his case. In the end, the overlap between the Council of Europe and OSCE will remain limited for the most part because the OSCE participating states in North America and Central Asia will remain outside the Council of Europe.

Relations between the OSCE and UN have become more frequent since the end of the Cold War. The two organizations overlap in their key aims of security and cooperation. The OSCE fits within the category of a regional organization laid out in Chapter VIII of the UN Charter. In 1993, the OSCE received observer status at the UN. In the same year, the Swedish CiO instigated annual tripartite meetings between the OSCE, the Council of Europe and the UN organs based in Geneva, such as the United Nations High Commissioner for Refugees (UNHCR). These meetings focus on issues such as the rule of law, threats to security, and the international role in the former Yugoslavia. More recently, following the 11 September terrorist attacks, the OSCE and UN have worked together on issues dealing with the threat of terrorism in the OSCE area. There is also a close cooperation in the field. For example, the UN is active in Bosnia, Kosovo, and Georgia, running the international response to Abkhazia in the latter case. With the OSCE active in the former Yugoslavia as well as the "frozen conflicts," there is considerable room for cooperation. Nevertheless, relations on the ground may not be always so straightforward. For instance, there have been complaints among OSCE staff working in some missions over the failure of the UN to engage more with the OSCE.[8] These problems notwithstanding, the relationship between the OSCE and UN has developed significantly particularly in terms of the relations between the upper echelon of each organization. As we will discuss, the UN has even turned to the OSCE as an innovative model of an organization for regional security and cooperation.[9] Overall, the OSCE's ability to establish constructive relationships with all of these organizations bodes well for its future role in the European security architecture.

Conclusion

This chapter has offered two arguments that help define the OSCE's role in the Euro-Atlantic area. First, as the period of Détente defined the Helsinki Final Act and thus the CSCE, the post-Cold War era has shaped the OSCE. As we saw in Chapters 4 and 5, many of Europe's conflicts began at the same time as the OSCE was attempting to institutionalize mechanisms of security management. Similarly, as democratization and security have been more closely tied together, the OSCE has increasingly focused on democracy and human rights as its core objectives. Second, the OSCE is limited in its ability to shape the European security architecture. This limitation is more the result of a lack of political will and consensus than any regional factor. Thus, the OSCE has made its biggest impact in areas where it works alongside other organizations like the EU, NATO, the Council of Europe, and the UN. Nevertheless, the OSCE remains an important organization in areas that are outside the EU, NATO, and the Council of Europe, such as in Central Asia. As argued in the next chapter, the OSCE remains important because we continue to have outsiders in the Euro-Atlantic area.

7   Crisis? What crisis?

This book has argued that the OSCE has had an important role to play in the European security architecture. The previous chapters have illustrated how the OSCE works as an organization and how it affects the region. Finally, we look at the current opportunities and challenges for the OSCE. Words such as "crisis" and "decline" have recently been used to describe the organization. To what degree are these accurate descriptions of the OSCE? Our final argument is that the OSCE is neither in "crisis" nor "decline," but instead represents two important aspects of the European security architecture missing in other organizations: inclusion and communication. The relevance of the OSCE is further highlighted in this chapter as other regions begin to contemplate their own OSCE-like organizations. Overall, the OSCE will continue to hold an important place in the European security architecture as long as there are both insiders and outsiders in the Euro-Atlantic area.

This book has shown the origin, stasis, expansion, and regional engagement of the CSCE/OSCE. Since 1975, the conference/organization has played an important part, at times great and at times small, in the European security architecture. The OSCE has not developed into a new all-inclusive NATO as was the hope of the Russian Federation in the 1990s.[1] Nor has it always been the most effective regional organization in preventing conflict, building peace or keeping the peace. Although it has the mandate to employ a peace-keeping force, it has never done so and most likely never will, given the EU's entrance into the peace-keeping business, beginning with FYR Macedonia in March 2003. Member-states of other European organizations do not give the OSCE the same attention as they do NATO, the EU, or the Council of Europe. While this book in general, and this chapter specifically, has offered an argument for the continued relevance of the OSCE in the European security architecture, others have used words such as "crossroads," "decline" or "crisis" to describe the OSCE since the late 1990s.

Pál Dunay has recently presented a convincing case for why the OSCE may be in "crisis."[2] Dunay's argument is based on several factors. First, he argues that despite the Cold War "heyday" for the CSCE, the OSCE is no longer a visible organization among the other European organizations. There is no doubt that "west of Vienna" knowledge of the OSCE is indeed low, as this author can attest. At the same time, "east of Vienna" the OSCE remains one of the most visible regional organizations. Second, the OSCE is in crisis because it has been unable to adapt to the changing nature of the European security "landscape." Dunay argues that since 2001, the greatest threat to European security has been terrorism. While NATO, and to a lesser extent, the EU have been able to adapt to this new landscape, the OSCE has been restricted by the opposing political wills within the organization. Indeed, the OSCE's ability to adapt to changing situations is lessened by its need for political consensus in decision-making. Consensus is required for action at summits, Ministerial Councils, and at the PC, although this is not the case for other organizations in the OSCE, as Russia, for example, knows all too well. However, the argument that the OSCE is in crisis because terrorism is now the main threat to European security is misguided. Granted, terrorism is a major source of insecurity in Europe, but a prioritization of threats should be based on likely outcomes. The potential for ethnic conflict in the OSCE area, for example, among the Gagauz in Moldova or Abkhazia in Georgia, remains a real threat while those most likely to suffer from terrorism are outside the OSCE area. NATO has been able to engage the "War on Terrorism" because it has the capacity and political will to operate "out-of-area." What purpose would the OSCE have in engaging other regions in this way? Furthermore, prioritizing traditional security threats over other societal and human insecurities underestimates the impact that other sources of insecurity do pose. For instance, the EU, the Council of Europe and the OSCE have devoted significant resources to combating the trafficking of human beings. The UN Office on Drugs and Crime has shown how human trafficking remains a major problem in Eastern Europe and the former Soviet Union.[3]

Finally, and perhaps most convincingly, Dunay argues that the stalemate between the United States and its allies and the Russian Federation and its allies over reform in the OSCE is perpetuating an ineffective institution. Many Western governments have been keen to use the OSCE as a way to bring about change in the East. This political will has been expressed most clearly in the construction of the human dimension institutions in the OSCE such as the ODIHR and the FOM. Russia is keen to see the OSCE change, to move away from democratization and return to promoting CSBMs as the organization did in the Cold War.[4] American and Russian intransigence about reforms in the OSCE has little bearing on the OSCE's ability to play a greater role in the European security architecture. Issues of reform surround professionalism, the budget, years of personnel service, and the role of ODIHR in transitioning states. Overall, there is little indication that the OSCE area does not require an inclusive organization that promotes security and cooperation between and within states. No doubt the relevance of the OSCE in Western Europe has changed over the years. This may change as the OSCE begins to balance its regional bias to include Western Europe and North America as ODIHR has already begun doing. At the same time, there is no doubt that in some areas, the OSCE is needed "now more than ever."[5] Importantly, Dunay is not trying to write off the OSCE, but instead draw attention to it within the EU security community. As he states at the beginning of his argument, the EU needs a worthwhile OSCE. Despite changes since the end of the Cold War and the increasing organizational overlap between the OSCE and other regional organizations, if the OSCE did not exist, we would have to create it.

The OSCE does remain a relevant organization in the European security architecture. This book has illustrated that since 1975, the CSCE and then OSCE have played a particular role in the Euro-Atlantic area that revolves around political communication. If the OSCE were only a "talking box" that contained every nation from Vancouver to Vladivostok, then it would be an important organization nonetheless. This book has shown, however, that the OSCE means much more. In the post-Cold War era, the OSCE remains important in terms of epistemic input, quiet diplomacy, a focus on national minorities and its presence in the field, especially in the "frozen conflicts." The future of the OSCE will depend on the threats to security and the level of instability primarily in the post-Soviet area. Outside of the Baltic States, post-Soviet states remain in many cases unstable and undemocratic. While some states have moved toward democracy and the market since 1991, such as Russia and Ukraine, there remain critical uncertainties in these states and in the wider region. To date, only the Baltic States have achieved stable, secure, democratic statehood. Along with the other European organizations, the OSCE still has much to do in the Euro-Atlantic area.

The most recent example of the OSCE's relevance to the European security architecture is the role played by the organization in the "Russian Spy Case" in Georgia in September/October 2006. In September, Georgian officials charged four Russians with spying, including a charge of hiring locals to retrieve information on Georgia–NATO relations. Georgian officials arrested and charged the Russians as "spies" and surrounded a Russian military compound with police officers in an effort to prevent anyone from leaving. As expected, the Russian government deplored the action. Based on our discussion of Georgian-Russian relations over South Ossetia in Chapter 4, we know that bilateral relations have been poor, especially since Saakashvili was elected Georgian President in 2003. The Russian government responded by blocking trade, transport links, and financial transactions with Georgia. The OSCE was able to step into the dispute as a third actor and mediate between the groups. In particular, the 2006 CiO, Belgian Foreign Minister Karel De Gucht, was able to mediate the transfer of those arrested into the hands of the OSCE on 2 October. The OSCE is also the primary organization that will have to help Georgian-Russian relations become more constructive. While the OSCE has been the main organization in the dispute, it was not the only one. Perhaps unsurprisingly given the organization and the fact that the CiO is also an EU foreign minister, the EU also had a diplomatic role to play in pressuring the Georgian government to release the four arrested. Nevertheless, the OSCE is important because both states fall outside the EU and NATO; the two regional organizations that also manage security in the larger region. The Euro-Atlantic area is not finished with the OSCE.

The OSCE may also have a role to play outside of the OSCE area. We have already discussed the OSCE's widening relevance in areas contiguous to the OSCE area, such as in the case of the OSCE Election Support in Afghanistan. Furthermore, in the field of regional organizations, the OSCE remains unique because of its focus on "common and comprehensive" security. The OSCE's basic principles and mechanisms have not gone unnoticed. The threats to security and cooperation in the Euro-Atlantic area are not specific to the region. Other regions also have many of the same problems that the CSCE faced in the Cold War and the OSCE faces in the post-Cold War/ September 11 era. Masahiko Asada and more recently Craig Dunkerley argue that the CSBMs promoted in the Final Act and the CSCE are ideal for the Cold War-esque relations in East Asia.[6] Confidence-building measures are key to mediating between a rising China and a wary Japan as well as bringing Korean-Japanese relations closer. Security-building measures are important to promote peace and stability over the nuclear North Korea issue. Dunkerley adds that the common and comprehensive nature of security in the OSCE is an ideal approach to insecurities in East Asia.[7] Formalized political communication in

East Asia along the lines of the early CSCE would be a proven method to bring about security and cooperation in the region.

Individual institutions within the OSCE have also attracted attention from the outside world. For example, the HCNM has been recommended as an institution to emulate at the international level in the UN as well as the regional level in ASEAN and the Organization for African Unity.[8] Deteriorating state–minority relations are a sure way to conflict, as we have seen from the renewed fighting in Sri Lanka between the government and the Liberation Tigers of Tamil Eelam or the genocide in Rwanda in 1994. The UN needs a mechanism of conflict prevention that is more nuanced and personal than the UN Security Council. As is often the case, such as in Darfur in Sudan, the ability of the international community to act comes only after fighting has begun, and even sometimes not then. Conflict prevention through quiet diplomacy along the lines of the HCNM could offer an international approach to state–minority relations which is sadly lacking in today's security organizations. The question is whether other states would be willing to agree to the formation of an instrument such as the HCNM, even if it were only political rather than legal. For example, officials within the HCNM have stated that African states are wary of any momentum towards institutionalizing a supranational actor that would challenge national sovereignty. Then, again, perhaps Africa is not the place to start emulating the CSCE/OSCE. The political will must be there first. Nevertheless, the OSCE does have much to offer other organizations and other regions. Its relevance in the Euro-Atlantic since 1975 suggests that the CSCE/OSCE is an important development in dealing with security and cooperation in general.

This book has given an account of the CSCE/OSCE since its beginnings in early Soviet foreign policy to the OSCE's latest roles in the former Soviet Union and Yugoslavia. We saw in Chapter 1 how the CSCE/OSCE sits within a thick web of organizations that engage in security and cooperation in Europe. Not only does the OSCE have to contend with these organizations, but also with participating states, who are often members of some, if not all, other organizations, and these states decide how to play the organizations to their own benefit. As the organizations' priorities have increasingly converged, it becomes harder to disentangle the role of the OSCE from the other organizations. Hopefully, this book has offered clarification. In Chapter 2, we saw how the CSCE moved from Soviet foreign policy to consolidate the post-war status quo to Western initiatives of dialogue with the Socialist bloc. This chapter also illustrated how the CSCE Final Act had an impact on the Cold War only insofar as participating states had the willingness to comply with its political mandates. The end of Détente was a challenge to the Final Act's approach to security and cooperation.

However, the rise of Gorbachev in the Soviet Union, the fall of socialist regimes in Central and Eastern Europe and the subsequent end of the Cold War brought about a changed security landscape in Europe. The CSCE adapted to this change by institutionalizing and broadening the principles of the Final Act, as seen in Chapter 3. This institutionalization saw the creation of a myriad of institutions to engage the new challenges to European security and cooperation and added to the overall European security architecture. Chapter 4 illustrated how the OSCE has engaged with conflict in the former Soviet Union and Yugoslavia, paying special attention to the three "frozen conflicts" under OSCE mandate. We saw how the OSCE has approached conflict prevention and peace-building in the region. Chapter 5 focused on the OSCE's approach to democratization and human rights in the Euro-Atlantic. The case studies provide an illustration of ODIHR, the HCNM, and the FOM in action. Both Chapters 4 and 5 gave a special focus on the field activities of the OSCE, perhaps the organization's most important asset. Finally, Chapter 6 has offered an argument for the continued relevance of the OSCE in the Euro-Atlantic area. As long as there are insiders and outsiders among the other organizations in Europe, the OSCE will remain a vital part of the European security architecture.

Notes

Foreword

1 Julian Lindley-French, *NATO* (London: Routledge, 2007).
2 David J. Galbreath, *Nation-Building and Minority Politics in Post-Socialist States: Interests, Influence and Identities in Estonia and Latvia* (Stuttgart: Ibidem-Verlag, 2005).

Introduction

1 John Lewis Gaddis, *The Cold War* (New York: Allen Lane, 2005). Emphasis added.
2 For example, see Janie Leatherman, *From Cold War to Democratic Peace: Third Parties, Peaceful Change, and the OSCE* (Syracuse, NY: Syracuse University Press, 2003), and Gregory Flynn and Henry Farrell, "Piecing Together the Democratic Peace: The CSCE, Norms, and 'Construction' of Security in Post-Cold War Europe," *International Organization* 53, no. 3 (1999): 505–535.

1 European security and cooperation in context

1 For a general review of the major developments of the Cold War before Détente, see Colin Brown and Peter Mooney, *Cold War to Détente* (London: Heinemann Educational Books, 1976), and David Rees, *The Age of Containment* (Basingstoke: Macmillan, 1967).
2 See Jerry F. Hough and Merle Fainsod, *How the Soviet Union is Governed* (New York: Harvard University Press, 1979).
3 John Lewis Gaddis, *Strategies of Containment: A Critical Appraisal of Postwar American National Security Policy* (Oxford: Oxford University Press, 1982).
4 John W. Young and John Kent, *International Relations since 1945: A Global History* (Oxford: Oxford University Press, 2004), 441.
5 The policy of *Ostpolitik* (1972) was the foreign policy of the government headed by the West German Chancellor Willy Brandt (Social Democrat). This policy was only possible after the Social Democrats were able to defeat the Christian Democrats in the 1969 West German *Bundestag* election.
6 Robert O. Keohane, "International Organization and the Crisis of Interdependence," *International Organization* 29, no. 2 (1975): 357–365.

7 Robert Keohane and Joseph Nye, *Power and Interdependence: World Politics in Transition* (New York: Little Brown, 1977).
8 See Andrew Moravcsik, *The Choice for Europe* (London: Routledge, 1998).
9 See Toumas Forsberg, "Russia's Relationship with NATO: A Qualitative Change or Old Wine in New Bottles?," *Journal of Communist Studies and Transition Politics* 21, no. 3 (2005): 332–355.

2 The Helsinki Final Act and comprehensive security

1 On nonbinding agreements, see Oscar Schachter, "The Twilight Existence of Nonbinding International Agreements," *American Journal of International Law* 71, no. 2 (1977): 296–304.
2 Pertti Joenniemi, "The Challenges of 'New' and 'Old': The Case of Europe's North," in *The Baltic States and their Region: New Europe or Old?*, ed. David J. Smith (Amsterdam: Rodopi, 2005), 67–86.
3 Pekka Sivonen, "European Security: New, Old and Borrowed," *Journal of Peace Research* 27, no. 4 (1990): 385–397.
4 John Lewis Gaddis, *The Long Peace: Inquiries into the History of the Cold War* (New York: Oxford University Press, 1987).
5 Harold S. Russell, "The Helsinki Declaration: Brobdingnag or Lilliput?," *American Journal of International Law* 70, no. 2 (1976): 244.
6 See George Kennan, "The Source of Soviet Conduct," *Foreign Affairs* 25, no. 6 (1947): 566–582, and John Lewis Gaddis, *Strategies of Containment: A Critical Appraisal of Postwar American National Security Policy* (Oxford: Oxford University Press, 1982).
7 See Robert F. Byrnes, "United States Policy Towards Eastern Europe: Before and after Helsinki," *The Review of Politics* 37, no. 4 (1975): 435–463.
8 See Christopher D. Jones, *Soviet Influence in Eastern Europe: Political Autonomy and the Warsaw Pact* (Brooklyn, NY: Praeger, 1981), and David Holloway and Jane M. O. Sharp, *The Warsaw Pact: Alliance in Transition?* (London: Macmillan, 1984).
9 See J. E. S. Fawcett, "The Council of Europe and Integration," *International Affairs* 50, no. 2 (1974): 242–250.
10 Russell, "The Helsinki Declaration: Brobdingnag or Lilliput?," 244.
11 See Robert Litwak, *Detente and the Nixon Doctrine: American Foreign Policy and the Pursuit of Stability, 1969–1976* (Cambridge: Cambridge University Press, 1984), and Raymond L. Garthoff, *Detente and Confrontation: American-Soviet Relations from Nixon to Reagan* (Washington, DC: Brookings Institution Press, 1985).
12 Note that the countries of the European Community worked together as a political entity at the CSCE negotiations and have continued to do so since. Arguably, member-state cooperation at the CSCE negotiations is an early example of a common foreign and security policy (CFSP).
13 On perspectives on Détente, see J. I. Coffey, "Detente, Arms Control and European Security," *International Affairs (Royal Institute of International Affairs 1944–)* 52, no. 1 (1976): 39–52.
14 Russell, "The Helsinki Declaration: Brobdingnag or Lilliput?"
15 Ibid., 242.
16 Ibid., 246.

17 Ibid., 246, emphasis added.
18 Robert Legvold, "Containment without Confrontation," *Foreign Policy* 40, (1980): 74–98.
19 Russell, "The Helsinki Declaration: Brobdingnag or Lilliput?," 251.
20 Ibid., 251.
21 Robert Putnam, "Diplomacy and Domestic Politics: The Logic of Two-Level Games," *International Organization* Summer, (1988): 467–469.
22 Russell, "The Helsinki Declaration: Brobdingnag or Lilliput?," 250.
23 CSCE Helsinki Final Act is available at www.osce.org/item/4046.html.
24 Russell, "The Helsinki Declaration: Brobdingnag or Lilliput?," 263.
25 CSCE Helsinki Final Act 1975, 4.
26 Russell, "The Helsinki Declaration: Brobdingnag or Lilliput?," 264.
27 Ibid., 251.
28 Ibid., 265.
29 Ibid., 265.
30 Itar-Tass, 28 April 2005.
31 Russell, "The Helsinki Declaration: Brobdingnag or Lilliput?," 266.
32 Ibid.
33 Ibid., 255.
34 Ibid., 268.
35 See Julie A. Mertus, *United Nations and Human Rights* (London: Routledge, 2005).
36 Russell, "The Helsinki Declaration: Brobdingnag or Lilliput?," 269.
37 See Rogers Brubaker, *Nationalism Reframed: Nationhood and the National Question in the New Europe* (Cambridge: Cambridge University Press, 1996), and Jennifer Jackson Preece, *National Minorities and the European Nation-States System* (Oxford: Clarendon Press, 1998).
38 Dimitri Simes, "The Death of Detente?," *International Security* 5, no. 1 (1980): 3–25.
39 Volker Rittberger, Manfred Efinger and Martin Mendler, "Toward an East-West Security Regime: The Case of Confidence- and Security-Building Measures," *Journal of Peace Research* 27, no. 1 (1990): 55–74.
40 Philip Hanson, "Economic Aspects of Helsinki," *International Affairs (Royal Institute of International Affairs 1944–)* 61, no. 4 (1985): 619–629.
41 John Galtung, "Violence, Peace and Peace Research," *Journal of Peace Research* 6, no. 3 (1969): 167–191.
42 Russell, "The Helsinki Declaration: Brobdingnag or Lilliput?," 260.
43 Longin Pastusiak, "Objective and Subjective Premises of Detente," *Journal of Peace Research* 14, no. 2 (1977): 185–193.
44 Mike Bowker and Phil Williams, "Helsinki and West European Security," *International Affairs* 61, no. 4 (1985): 607–618.
45 CSCE Helsinki Final Act 1975.
46 Sivonen, "European Security: New, Old and Borrowed," 388.
47 Brian Fall, "The Helsinki Conference, Belgrade and European Security," *International Security* 2, no. 1 (1977): 100–105.
48 Fred Chernoff, "Negotiating Security and Disarmament in Europe," *International Affairs* 60, no. 3 (1984): 429–437.
49 Dante B. Fascell, "The Helsinki Accord: A Case Study," *The Annals of the American Academy of Political and Social Science* 442, *The Human Dimension of Foreign Policy: An American Perspective* (1979): 71.

50 Dante B. Fascell, "Did Human Rights Survive Belgrade?," *Foreign Policy* no. 31 (1978): 105–107.
51 Ibid., 107.
52 Stephen Van Evera, "Primed for Peace: Europe after the Cold War," *International Security* 15, no. 3 (1991): 7–57.

3 From "Conference" to "Organization"

1 See Jerry F. Hough and Merle Fainsod, *How the Soviet Union is Governed* (New York: Harvard University Press, 1979), and Richard D. Little, *Governing the Soviet Union* (London: Longman, 1989).
2 See Michael E. Brown, Sean M. Lynn-Jones and Steven E. Miller, eds, *Debating the Democratic Peace* (Cambridge, MA: MIT Press, 1996).
3 Edward D. Mansfield and Jack Snyder, "Democratization and the Danger of War," *International Security* 20, no. 1 (1995): 5–38, and Michael Doyle, "Liberalism and World Politics," *American Political Science Review* 80, no. 4 (1983): 1151–1169, and Bruce M. Russett, *Grasping the Democratic Peace: Principles for a Post-Cold War World* (Princeton, NJ: Princeton University Press, 1993), and Edward D. Mansfield and Jack Snyder, "Democratic Transitions, Institutional Strength, and War," *International Organization* 56, no. 2 (2002): 297–337, and David J. Galbreath, "Democratisation and Inter-State War: Why Reform Does Not Encourage Conflict," *Politics* 24, no. 3 (2004): 212–220.
4 See Andrew Moravcsik, *The Choice for Europe* (London: Routledge, 1998), and Jon C. Pevehouse, "Democracy from the Outside-In? International Organizations and Democratization," *International Organization* 56, no. 3 (2002): 515–549.
5 Wolfgang Merkel, "Embedded and Defective Democracies," *Democratization* 11, no. 5 (2004): 33–58.
6 Rogers Brubaker, *Nationalism Reframed: Nationhood and the National Question in the New Europe* (Cambridge: Cambridge University Press, 1996).
7 Tove H. Malloy, *National Minority Rights in Europe* (Oxford: Oxford University Press, 2005).
8 Jane I. Dawson, *Eco-Nationalism: Anti-Nuclear Activism and National Identity in Russia, Lithuania, and Ukraine* (London: Duke University Press, 1996).
9 For example, see Juris Dreifelds, "Two Latvian Dams: Two Confrontations," *Baltic Forum* 6, no. 1 (1989): 11–24.
10 See Juan J. Linz and Alfred Stepan, *Problems of Democratic Transition and Consolidation: Southern Europe, South America, and Post-Communist Europe* (Baltimore, MD: Johns Hopkins University Press, 1996).
11 *OSCE Handbook* (Vienna: Secretariat of the OSCE, 1999).
12 Jennifer Jackson Preece, *National Minorities and the European Nation-States System* (Oxford: Clarendon Press, 1998), 28.
13 The name change came into force on 1 January 1995.
14 OSCE Permanent Council Declaration PC.DEC/364.
15 Much of the information on the current CiO is based on an interview in the Belgian Delegation to the OSCE. The author would like to show his special appreciation of the Deputy Permanent Representative of Belgium of the OSCE, Pascal Heyman.

16 *Foreign Policy of Belgium: Organization for Security and Co-Operation in Europe (OSCE)*. The Belgian Chairmanship of the OSCE in 2006 (Background paper approved by the Council of Ministers on 3 December 2005) www.osce.org/item/17710.html (accessed 16 June 2006).
17 Much of the information on the HCNM is based on author interviews in The Hague.
18 When referring to the senior office specifically, I use the term "High Commissioner" and use "HCNM" to denote the institution as a whole. Wolfgang Zellner, *On the Effectiveness of the OSCE Minority Regime: Comparative Case Studies on Implementation of the Recommendations of the High Commissioner on National Minorities of the OSCE* (Hamburg: Hamburger Beiträge zur Friedensforschung und Sicherheitspolitik, Heft, 1999), and Rob Zaagman, *Conflict Prevention in the Baltic States: The OSCE High Commissioner on National Minorities in Estonia, Latvia, and Lithuania* (Flensburg: European Centre for Minority Issues, 1999), and Walter A. Kemp, *Quiet Diplomacy in Action: The OSCE High Commissioner on National Minorities* (The Hague: Kluwer Law International, 2001).
19 In an interview with the author, the current OSCE High Commissioner, Ambassador Rolf Ekeus, stated that despite an initial interest from the African Union, member-states were highly skeptical of such an institution in Africa. See Rianne Letschert, "Towards a UN Representative on Minority Issues: Drawing upon the Experiences of the OSCE High Commissioner on National Minorities," *Helsinki Monitor* 13, no. 4 (2002): 326–337.
20 Randolf Oberschmidt, "Office for Democratic Institutions and Human Rights: An Interim Appraisal," *Helsinki Monitor* 12, no. 4 (2001): 278.
21 Ibid., 280.
22 Ibid., 281.
23 The relationship between the OSCE and the Council of Europe continues to grow. See *Co-operation between the Organization for Security and Co-operation in Europe and the Council of Europe* (PC Decision No. 670) www.osce.org/item/14103.html (accessed 17 June 2006).
24 Information is based on the author's interview with officials at the OSCE FOM in Vienna.
25 Regular Report to the Permanent Council by the OSCE Representative on Freedom of the Media on 15 December 2005.
26 Regular Report to the Permanent Council by the OSCE Representative on Freedom of the Media on 16 February 2006.
27 Ana Karlsreiter and Hanna Vuokko, eds, *Ending the Chilling Effect: Working to Repeal Criminal Libel and Insult Laws* (Vienna: OSCE Representative on Freedom of the Media, 2004).
28 Christian Möller and Arnaud Armouroux, eds, *The Media Freedom Internet Cookbook* (Vienna: OSCE Representative on Freedom of the Media, 2004).
29 Freimut Duve and Michael Haller, eds, *Editorial Independence: Putting Principle into Practice* (Vienna: OSCE Representative on Freedom of the Media, 2005).
30 See OSCE Secretariat, *Survey of OSCE Long-term Missions and Other OSCE Field Activities* (Vienna: Conflict Prevention Centre, 2005).

31 Ibid., 7–8.
32 Ibid., 10.
33 David J. Galbreath, *Nation-Building and Minority Politics in Post-Socialist States: Interests, Influence and Identities in Estonia and Latvia* (Stuttgart: Ibidem Verlag, 2005), 260–261.
34 OSCE Secretariat, *Survey of OSCE Long-term Missions and Other OSCE Field Activities*, 77.
35 Ibid., 48, emphasis added.
36 Information provided at author's interview in the OSCE HCNM, The Hague, 31 March 2006.
37 See OSCE Office for Democratic Institutions and Human Rights, *Summary Report: OSCE/ODIHR Expert Meeting on Election Observation*, Moscow, 22–23 November 2005, 8.
38 M. J. Peterson, *The United Nations General Assembly* (London: Routledge, 2005).
39 Information based on interviews in delegations from the UK, Belgium, the Russian Federation, Estonia and Latvia.
40 Robert Putnam, "Diplomacy and Domestic Politics: The Logic of Two-Level Games," *International Organization* Summer, (1988): 427–461.
41 Information based on interviews at the OSCE Forum for Security Co-operation in Vienna, 18 May 2006.
42 See Wade Jacoby, *The Enlargement of the European Union and NATO: Ordering from the Menu in Central Europe* (Cambridge: Cambridge University Press, 2004), 116–178.
43 FSC Decision No. 15/02 Expert Advice on Implementation of Section V of the OSCE Document on Small Arms and Light Weapons.
44 Ibid.
45 For example, see Markus Jachtenfuchs, "Deepening and Widening Integration Theory," *Journal of European Public Policy* 9, no. 4 (2002): 650–657.
46 See Marianne Hanson, "Russia and NATO Expansion: The Uneasy Basis of the Founding Act," *European Security* 7, no. 2 (1998): 13–29, and Henning Sorensen, "NATO and its New Military Security Position," *European Security* 7, no. 1 (1998): 74–79.
47 Jeff Chinn and Robert Kaiser, *Russians as the New Minority: Ethnicity and Nationalism in the Soviet Successor States* (Boulder, CO: Westview Press, 1996), and Pål Kolstø, *Russians in the Former Soviet Republics* (London: Hurst, 1995), and Neil J. Melvin, *Russians beyond Russia: The Politics of National Identity* (London: Royal Institute of International Affairs, 1995).
48 Galbreath, *Nation-Building and Minority Politics in Post-Socialist States: Interests, Influence and Identities in Estonia and Latvia*, 189–232.
49 M. Steven Fish, *Democracy Derailed in Russia: The Failure of Open Politics* (Cambridge: Cambridge University Press, 2005).

4 Security management

1 See Johan Galtung, "Violence, Peace and Peace Research," *Journal of Peace Research* 6, no. 3 (1969): 167–191.
2 See Barry Buzan, Ole Waever and Jaap de Wilde, *Security: A New Framework for Analysis* (Boulder, CO: Lynne Rienner, 1998), and Barry

Buzan, "Security Architecture in Asia: The Interplay of Regional and Global Levels," *The Pacific Review* 16, no. 2 (2003): 143–173.

3 Interview by the author of the OSCE High Commissioner on National Minorities, The Hague, 31 March 2006.

4 Jonathan Cohen, *Conflict Prevention in the OSCE: An Assessment of Capacities* (The Hague: Netherlands Institute of International Relations, 1999), 12.

5 Elisa Niemtzow, "The OSCE's Security Model: Conceptual Confusion and Competing Visions," *Helsinki Monitor* 7, no. 3 (1996): 41.

6 For example, see Sven Biscop, *The European Security Strategy: A Global Agenda for Positive Power* (Aldershot: Ashgate, 2005).

7 Niemtzow, "The OSCE's Security Model: Conceptual Confusion and Competing Visions," 42.

8 Several authors have looked at Russia's expectations for the OSCE, see Heather Hulbert, "Russia, the OSCE and European Security Architecture," *Helsinki Monitor* 6, no. 2 (1995): 5–20; Niemtzow, "The OSCE's Security Model: Conceptual Confusion and Competing Visions," 41–51; Victor-Yves Ghebali, "The Russian Factor in OSCE Crisis: A Fair Examination," *Helsinki Monitor* 16, no. 3 (2005): 184–187; Wolfgang Zellner, "Russia and the OSCE: From High Hopes to Disillusionment," *Cambridge Review of International Affairs* 18, no. 3 (2005): 389–402; and Edith Drieskens, "Playing the Russian Card: The Belgian OSCE Chairmanship," *Helsinki Monitor* 17, no. 1 (2006): 1–3.

9 P. Terrence Hopmann, "Managing Conflict in Post-Cold War Eurasia: The Role of the OSCE in Europe's Security Architecture," *International Politics* 40, no. 1 (2003): 79–85, and P. Terrence Hopmann, "The OSCE Role in Eurasian Security," in *Limiting Institutions? The Challenge of Eurasian Security Governance*, eds James Sperling, Sean Kay and S. Victor Papacosma (Manchester: Manchester University Press, 2003), 144–165.

10 Christer Pusiainen, "The Impact of International Security Regimes on Russia's Behavior: The Case of the OSCE and Chechnya," in *Understandings of Russian Foreign Policy* (University Park, PA: Pennsylvania State University Press, 1999), and Pavel K. Baev, "Russia's Stance against Secessions: From Chechnya to Kosovo," *International Peacekeeping* 6, no. 3 (1999): 73–94.

11 See Dmitri V. Trenin, Aleksei V. Malashenko and Anatol Lieven, *Russia's Restless Frontier: The Chechnya Factor in Post-Soviet Russia* (Washington, DC: Carnegie Endowment for International Peace, 2004).

12 Robert H. Frowick, "OSCE: in Bosnia and Beyond," *Cambridge Review of International Affairs* 11, no. 1 (1997): 92–103.

13 Michael Pugh and Margaret Cobble, "Non-Nationalist Voting in Bosnian Municipal Elections: Implications for Democracy and Peacebuilding," *Journal of Peace Research* 38, no. 1 (2001): 27–47.

14 See Andrea Kathryn Talentino, "Intervention as Nation-Building: Illusion or Possibility?," *Security Dialogue* 33, no. 1 (2002): 27–44.

15 Charles Krupnick, "Europe's Intergovernmental NGO: The OSCE in Europe's Emerging Security Structure," *European Security* 7, no. 2 (1998): 30–53.

16 Rogers Brubaker, *Nationalism Reframed: Nationhood and the National Question in the New Europe* (Cambridge: Cambridge University Press, 1996).

17 See Svante E. Cornell, "Turkey and the Conflict in Nagorno Karabakh: A Delicate Balance," *Middle Eastern Studies* 34, no. 1 (1998): 51–72, and Pavel K. Baev, "Russia's Policies in the Southern Caucasus and the Caspian Area," *European Security* 10, no. 2 (2001): 95–110.
18 See Stephan Astourian, "The Nagorno-Karabakh Conflict: Dimensions, Lessons, and Prospects," *Mediterranean Quarterly* 5, no. 4 (1994): 85–109; Terhi Hakala, "The OSCE Minsk Process: A Balance after Five Years," *Helsinki Monitor* 9, no. 1 (1998): 5–15; Moorad Mooradian, "The OSCE: Neutral and Impartial in the Karabakh Conflict," *Helsinki Monitor* 9, no. 2 (1998): 5–17; Maria Raquel Freire, *Conflict and Security in the Former Soviet Union: The Role of the OSCE* (Aldershot: Ashgate, 2003), and Maria Raquel Freire, "The Search for Innovative Procedures: The OSCE Approach to Conflicts in the Former Soviet Area," in *Sovereignty and the Global Community: The Quest for Order in the International System*, ed. Howard M. Hensel (Aldershot: Ashgate, 2004).
19 The meeting between ministers was the Helsinki Additional Meeting of the CSCE Council on 24 March 1992.
20 Hakala, "The OSCE Minsk Process: A Balance after Five Years," 5.
21 Ibid., 7.
22 Ibid., 11–12.
23 See especially, Mooradian, "The OSCE: Neutral and Impartial in the Karabakh Conflict," 5–17.
24 Jaba Devdariani, "Georgia and Russia: The Troubled Road to Accommodation," in *Statehood and Security: Georgia after the Rose Revolution*, eds Bruno Coppieters and Robert Legvold (London: MIT Press, 2005), 153–203.
25 See Monica Duffy Tuft, "Multinationality, Regional Institutions, State-Building, and the Failed Transition in Georgia," in *Ethnicity and Territory in the Former Soviet Union: Regions in Conflict*, eds James Hughes and Gwendolyn Sasse (London: Frank Cass, 2002), 123–142; David J. Galbreath, *Nation-Building and Minority Politics in Post-Socialist States: Interests, Influence and Identities in Estonia and Latvia* (Stuttgart: Ibidem Verlag, 2005), and David J. Galbreath, "From Nationalism to Nation-Building: Latvian Politics and Minority Policy," *Nationalities Papers* 34, no. 4 (2006): 383–406.
26 Jean-Michel Lacombe, "The OSCE Mission to Georgia: Mandate and Activities," in *The OSCE and the Multiple Challenges of Transition*, eds Farian Sabahi and Daniel Warner (Aldershot: Ashgate, 2004), 161–168.
27 Megumi Nishimura, "The OSCE and Ethnic Conflicts in Estonia, Georgia and Tajikistan: A Search for Sustainable Peace and Its Limits," *European Security* 8, no. 1 (1999): 33–35.
28 OSCE Secretariat, *Survey of OSCE Long-term Missions and Other OSCE Field Activities* (Vienna: Conflict Prevention Centre, 2005), 11–12.
29 See Bruno Coppieters and Robert Legvold, eds, *Statehood and Security: Georgia after the Rose Revolution* (London: MIT Press, 2005).
30 Ghia Nodia, "Georgia: Dimensions of Insecurity," in *Statehood and Security: Georgia after the Rose Revolution*, eds Bruno Coppieters and Robert Legvold (London: MIT Press, 2005).
31 See Neil J. Melvin, *Russians beyond Russia: The Politics of National Identity* (London: Royal Institute of International Affairs, 1995), and

David D. Laitin, *Identity in Formation: The Russian-Speaking Populations in the Near Abroad* (Ithaca, NY: Cornell University Press, 1998).

32 Alla Skvortsova, "The Cultural and Social Makeup of Moldova: A Bipolar or Dispersed Society," in *National Integration and Violent Conflict in Post-Soviet Societies: The Cases of Estonia and Moldova*, ed. Pål Kolstø (Oxford: Rowman and Littlefield, 2002).

33 Jonathan Eyal and Graham Smith, "Moldova and Moldovans," in *The Nationalities Question in the Post-Soviet States*, ed. Graham Smith (London: Longman, 1996), 223–244.

34 Freire, *Conflict and Security in the Former Soviet Union: The Role of the OSCE*, 197.

35 Ibid., 199.

36 Ibid., 202.

37 OSCE Secretariat, *Survey of OSCE Long-term Missions and Other OSCE Field Activities*, 16–18.

38 Author interview with the Russian delegation to the OSCE in Vienna, 18 May 2006.

39 Author interviews in the OSCE Conflict Prevention Centre, Vienna, 25 April–18 May 2006.

40 See Michael Mann, *The Dark Side of Democracy: Explaining Ethnic Cleansing* (Cambridge: Cambridge University Press, 2005), 353–427, and Duško Sekulić, Garth Massey and Randy Hodson, "Ethnic Intolerance and Ethnic Conflict in the Dissolution of Yugoslavia," *Ethnic and Racial Studies* 29, no. 5 (2006): 797–827.

41 Trevor Salmon, "Testing Times for European Political Cooperation: The Gulf and Yugoslavia, 1990–92," *International Affairs* 68, no. 2 (1992): 233–253.

42 James Dobbins, "The UN's Role in Nation-building: From the Belgian Congo to Iraq," *Survival* 46, no. 4 (2004): 81–102, and Ruth Wedgewood, "NATO's Campaign in Yugoslavia," *American Journal of International Law* 93, no. 4 (1999): 828–834.

43 The term "Bosniak" is officially used to describe Bosnian Muslims. The term "ethnic cleansing" was adopted from the Serbo-Croat phrase "etnicko ciscenje," thought to originate in the early 1980s to explain Kosovo Albanian aggression on Kosovo Serbs. See Drazen Petrovic, "Ethnic Cleansing: An Attempt at Methodology," *European Journal of International Law* 5, no. 3 (1994): 1–19.

44 Dov Lynch, "'Walking the Tightrope': The Kosovo Conflict and Russia in European Security," *European Security* 8, no. 4 (1999): 57–83, and Predrag Simic, "Russia and the Conflicts in the Former Yugoslavia," *Journal of Southeast European and Black Sea Studies* 1, no. 3 (2001): 95–114.

45 The OSCE Mission to Croatia mandate was first set out in April 1996 but was subsequently broadened in June 1997. The mission's mandate is based on Permanent Council Decisions No. 112 and No. 176. A previous short-term CSCE mission to Croatia and Bosnia-Herzegovina in 1992 was based on the "Moscow mechanism" which allows for a quick-response rapporteur mission to be deployed in emergency situations, see Cohen, *Conflict Prevention in the OSCE: An Assessment of Capacities*, 40–42.

46 See Thomas G. Weiss and David A. Korn, *Internal Displacement: Conceptualization and its Consequences* (London: Routledge, 2006).

47 Unfortunately for Poland, the Czech Republic and Hungary, these countries were participating in NATO sorties only a day after gaining membership in the North Atlantic alliance. Wedgewood, "NATO's Campaign in Yugoslavia," 828–834, and Stuart Croft, Jolyon Howorth, Terry Terriff and Mark Webber, "NATO's Triple Challenge," *International Affairs* 76, no. 3 (2000): 495–518.

48 See Alex J. Bellamy and Stuart Griffin, "OSCE Peacekeeping: Lessons from the Kosovo Verification Mission," *European Security* 11, no. 1 (2002): 1–26.

49 OSCE Secretariat, *Survey of OSCE Long-term Missions and Other OSCE Field Activities*, 25.

50 Andrew Taylor, "Electoral Systems and the Promotion of 'Consociationalism' in a Multi-ethnic Society: The Kosovo Assembly Elections of November 2001," *Electoral Studies* 24, no. 3 (2005): 435–463.

51 Katarina Mansson, "Cooperation in Human Rights: Experience from the Peace Operation in Kosovo," *International Peacekeeping* 8, no. 4 (2001): 111–135.

52 Valery Perry, "The OSCE Suspension of the Federal Republic of Yugoslavia," *Helsinki Monitor* 9, no. 4 (1998): 45.

53 Ibid., 46.

54 Ibid., 47.

55 OSCE Secretariat, *Survey of OSCE Long-term Missions and Other OSCE Field Activities*, 29.

5 Democratization and human rights

1 See Dimitri K. Simes, "Human Rights and Detente," *Proceedings of the Academy of Political Science* 33, no. 1, *The Soviet Threat: Myths and Realities* (1978): 135–147.

2 See Juan J. Linz and Alfred Stepan, *Problems of Democratic Transition and Consolidation: Southern Europe, South America, and Post-Communist Europe* (Baltimore, MD: Johns Hopkins University Press, 1996), and Charles Kurzman, "Waves of Democratization," *Studies in Comparative International Development* 33, no. 1 (1998): 42–64.

3 *Belgian Chairmanship* (Brussels: Belgian Ministry of Foreign Affairs, 2006), 15.

4 Geoffrey Edwards, "Human Rights and Basket III Issues: Areas of Change and Continuity," *International Affairs* 61, no. 4 (1985): 631–642, and Floribert Baudet, "The Origins of the CSCE Human Dimension Mechanism: A Case Study in Dutch Cold War Policy," *Helsinki Monitor* 12, no. 1 (2001): 185–196.

5 Dante B. Fascell, "Did Human Rights Survive Belgrade?," *Foreign Policy* no. 31 (1978): 104–118.

6 Ibid., 104.

7 Samuel P. Huntington, *The Third Wave* (Norman, OK: University of Oklahoma Press, 1991).

8 Edward D. Mansfield and Jack Snyder, "Democratization and the Danger of War," *International Security* 20, no. 1 (1995): 5–38, and Edward D. Mansfield and Jack Snyder, "Democratic Transitions, Institutional Strength, and War," *International Organization* 56, no. 2 (2002): 297–337.

9 Audrey Glover, "The Human Dimension of the OSCE: From Standard Setting to Implementation," *Helsinki Monitor* 6, no. 3 (1995): 31–39.

10 See ODIHR, *NGOs in the Caucasus and Central Asia: Development and Co-operation with the OSCE* (Warsaw: ODIHR, 2000).

11 Randolf Oberschmidt, "Office for Democratic Institutions and Human Rights – An Interim Appraisal," *Helsinki Monitor* 12, no. 4 (2001): 277–290.

12 Ibid., 278.

13 Ibid., 281.

14 Bruce Cronin, "Creating Stability in the New Europe: The OSCE High Commissioner on National Minorities and the Socialization of Risky States," *Security Studies* 12, no. 1 (2002): 132–163, and John Packer, "Confronting the Contemporary Challenges of Europe's Minorities," *Helsinki Monitor* 16, no. 2 (2005): 227–231.

15 Walter A. Kemp and Stefan Wolff, "Quiet Diplomacy in Action: The OSCE High Commissioner on National Minorities," *Nationalities Papers* 31, no. 3 (2003): 358–359.

16 Toomas Hendrik Ilves, "The OSCE Mission to Estonia," *Helsinki Monitor* 13, no. 4 (2002): 320–325.

17 For example, see the *Freedom and Responsibility: 2005 Yearbook of the Representative on Freedom of the Media* at www.osce.org/fom/item_11_20011.html

18 Charles King and Neil J. Melvin, *Nations Abroad: Diaspora Politics and International Relations in the Former Soviet Union* (Boulder, CO: Westview Press, 1998), and Neil J. Melvin, *Russians beyond Russia: The Politics of National Identity* (London: Royal Institute of International Affairs, 1995), and David D. Laitin, *Identity in Formation: The Russian-Speaking Populations in the Near Abroad* (Ithaca, NY: Cornell University Press, 1998).

19 Anatol Lievan, *The Baltic Revolution: Estonia, Latvia, Lithuania and the Path to Independence* (London: Yale University Press, 1993).

20 Ilga Apine, "Ethnic Policy in the Baltic States," in *The Baltic States: A Historical Crossroads*, ed. Talavs Jundzis (Riga: Latvian Academy of Sciences, 2001).

21 Not all the minorities in Latvia are Russians. There are considerable numbers of Ukrainians and Byelorussians as well as other smaller groups who are generally lumped together as Russian-speakers or Russophonic.

22 David J. Galbreath, "From Nationalism to Nation-Building: Latvian Politics and Minority Policy," *Nationalities Papers* 34, no. 4 (2006): 383–406.

23 Aadne Aasland, "Citizenship Status and Social Exclusion in Estonia and Latvia," *Journal of Baltic Studies* 23, no. 1 (2002): 57–77, and Mark A. Jubulis, *Nationalism and Democratic Transition: The Politics of Citizenship and Language in Post-Soviet Latvia* (New York: University Press of America, 2001).

24 Artis Pabriks and Aldis Purs, *Latvia: The Challenges of Change* (London: Routledge, 2002), 87.

25 See David J. Galbreath and Mary Elizabeth Galvin, "The Titularization of Latvian Secondary Schools: The Historical Legacy of Soviet Policy Implementation," *Journal of Baltic Studies* 4, no. 36 (2005): 449–466.

26 Note that there also exist other minority schools other than Russian, including Ukrainian and Polish. See Gabrielle Hogan-Brun, "The Baltic

Republics and Language Ideological Debates Surrounding European Union Accession," *Journal of Multilingual and Multicultural Development* 26, no. 5 (2005): 367–377, and Gabrielle Hogan-Brun, "At the Interface of Language Ideology and Practice: The Public Discourse Surrounding the 2004 Education Reform in Latvia," *Language Policy* 5, no. 2 (2006): 69–73, and Iveta Silova, *From Sites of Occupation to Symbols of Multiculturalism: Re-conceptualizing Minority Education in Post-soviet Latvia* (Greenwich, CT: Information Age Publishing, 2006).

27 David J. Galbreath, "The Politics of European Integration and Minority Rights in Estonia and Latvia," *Perspectives on European Politics and Society* 4, no. 1 (2003): 35–54, and David J. Galbreath, "European Integration through Democratic Conditionality: Latvia in the Context of Minority Rights," *Journal of Contemporary European Studies* 14, no. 1 (2006): 69–87.

28 CSCE Communication No. 124 and 125/Add.1.

29 Charles F. Furtado and Michael Hechter, "The Emergence of Nationalist Politics in the USSR: A Comparison of Estonia and the Ukraine," in *Thinking Theoretically about Soviet Nationalities: History and Comparison in the Study of the USSR*, ed. Alexander J. Motyl (New York: Columbia University Press, 1992), 169–204.

30 See Graham Smith and Andrew Wilson, "Rethinking Russia's Post-Soviet Diaspora: The Potential for Political Mobilization in Eastern Ukraine and North-East Estonia," *Europe-Asia Studies* 49, no. 5 (1997): 845–864.

31 Volodymyr Kulyk, "Revisiting a Success Story: Implementation of the Recommendations of the OSCE High Commissioner on National Minorities to Ukraine, 1994–2001," Centre for OSCE Research: CORE Working Paper (2002).

32 OSCE Secretariat, *Survey of OSCE Long-term Missions and Other OSCE Field Activities* (Vienna: Conflict Prevention Centre, 2005), 70–71.

33 Ibid., 43–44.

34 OSCE Mission to Kyrgyzstan Fact Sheet (www.osce.org/bishkek/item_11_19745.html).

35 The OSCE Mission to Bosnia and Herzegovina is one of the most expensive field missions. The 2005 budget was over € 16 million.

36 OSCE Mission to Bosnia and Herzegovina Fact Sheet (www.oscebih.org/documents/46-eng.pdf).

37 OSCE Spillover Monitor Mission to Skopje Fact Sheet (www.osce.org/skopje/item_11_13998.html).

38 OSCE Presence in Albania Fact Sheet (www.osce.org/albania/item_11_13546.html).

6 The OSCE and the European security architecture

1 Volker Rittberger, Manfred Efinger and Martin Mendler, "Toward an East-West Security Regime: The Case of Confidence- and Security-Building Measures," *Journal of Peace Research* 27, no. 1 (1990): 55–74.

2 Interview at the OSCE Secretariat in Vienna, 14 May 2006.

3 Information on OSCE external relations is largely based on interviews in the OSCE Secretariat External Co-operation Division and CPC in Vienna, 17–19 May 2006. See also www.osce.org/ec/.

4 Istanbul Summit Communiqué (www.nato.int/docu/pr/2004/p04–096e.htm)
5 Interview at the OSCE in Vienna, 17–19 May 2006.
6 Tove H. Malloy, *National Minority Rights in Europe* (Oxford: Oxford University Press, 2005).
7 David J. Galbreath, "European Integration through Democratic Conditionality: Latvia in the Context of Minority Rights," *Journal of Contemporary European Studies* 14, no. 1 (2006): 69–87.
8 Interview with OSCE field personnel in July 2006.
9 Rianne Letschert, "Towards a UN Representative on Minority Issues: Drawing upon the Experiences of the OSCE High Commissioner on National Minorities," *Helsinki Monitor* 13, no. 4 (2002): 326–337.

7 Crisis? What crisis?

1 Wolfgang Zellner, "Russia and the OSCE: From High Hopes to Disillusionment," *Cambridge Review of International Affairs* 18, no. 3 (2005): 389–402.
2 Pál Dunay, "The OSCE in Crisis," Institute for Security Studies, Chaillot Paper 88 (2006), and Robert L. Barry, *The Future of the OSCE* (London: British American Security Information Council, 2003), and Robert L. Barry, *The OSCE: A Forgotten Transatlantic Security Organisation?* (London: British American Security Information Council, 2002).
3 See UNODC Report "Trafficking in Human Beings: Global Patterns," April 2006 (www.unodc.org/unodc/en/trafficking_persons_report_2006–04.html).
4 Interviews with the Russian Delegation to the OSCE in Vienna, 17–19 May 2006.
5 Eric J. Mlyn, "OSCE: Now More than Ever," *Cambridge Review of International Affairs* XI, no. 2 (1998): 227–237.
6 Masahiko Asada, "Confidence-Building Measures in East Asia: A Japanese Perspective," *Asian Survey* 28, no. 5 (1988): 489–508, and Craig G. Dunkerley, "Considering Security amidst Strategic Change: The OSCE Experience," *Middle East Policy* 11, no. 3 (2004): 131–138.
7 Dunkerley, "Considering Security amidst Strategic Change: The OSCE Experience," 131–132.
8 Information based on interviews at the OSCE HCNM in The Hague, March 30, 2006.

Select bibliography

Jonathan Cohen, *Conflict Prevention in the OSCE: An Assessment of Capacities* (The Hague: Netherlands Institute of International Relations, 1999). Provides an in-depth discussion of the OSCE's mechanisms of conflict prevention, including a discussion of field activities.

Maria Raquel Freire, *Conflict and Security in the Former Soviet Union: The Role of the OSCE* (Aldershot: Ashgate, 2003). An insightful book on the role of the OSCE in the former Soviet Union, which offers an interesting set of case studies.

P. Terrence Hopmann, "Managing Conflict in Post-Cold War Eurasia: The Role of the OSCE in Europe's Security Architecture," *International Politics* 40, no. 1 (2003): 144–165. An article that brings together the mechanisms of security management in the Euro-Atlantic area.

Walter A. Kemp, *Quiet Diplomacy in Action: The OSCE High Commissioner on National Minorities* (The Hague: Kluwer Law International, 2001). A thorough account of the High Commissioner on National Minorities from inside the office.

Janie Leatherman, *From Cold War to Democratic Peace: Third Parties, Peaceful Change, and the OSCE* (Syracuse NY: Syracuse University Press, 2003). This book provides a link between the OSCE and the democratic peace theory, set within the context of post-Cold War Europe.

Michael Merlingen, "OSCE Studies: The State of the Art and Future Directions," *Journal of International Relations and Development* 6, no. 1 (2003): 71–85. A journal article that discusses the organization, following years of development. Merlingen provides a discussion of future prospects for the organization.

OSCE Handbook (Vienna: Secretariat of the OSCE, 1999). The organization's own publication, detailing its history and current activities. While basic, the Handbook offers great scope on the activities of the OSCE.

Harold S. Russell, "The Helsinki Declaration: Brobdingnag or Lilliput?," *American Journal of International Law* 70, no. 2 (1976): 242–272. A classic article detailing the bargaining of the Helsinki Process. Russell writes from inside the US delegation to the Helsinki Final Act.

Farian Sabahi and Daniel Warner, eds, *The OSCE and the Multiple Challenges of Transition* (Aldershot: Ashgate, 2004). An edited collection focusing on the OSCE's impact on political transition in the former Socialist bloc.

Daniel Warner, Victor-Yves Ghebali, Emeric Rogier and Marianne Rogier, eds, *The Operational Role of the OSCE in South-Eastern Europe: Contributing to Regional Stability in the Balkans* (Aldershot: Ashgate, 2001). An edited collection that looks at OSCE operations in the former Yugoslavia.

Wolfgang Zellner, "Russia and the OSCE: From High Hopes to Disillusionment," *Cambridge Review of International Affairs* 18, no. 3 (2005): 389–402. A defining article that details Russia's evolving relationship with the OSCE. Zellner offers consideration of the positive Yeltsin years as well as prospects for the future.

Index

GLOBAL INSTITUTIONS SERIES

NEW TITLE
United Nations Conference on Trade and Development (UNCTAD)

Ian Taylor, University of St Andrews, UK and
Karen Smith, University of Stellenbosch, South Africa

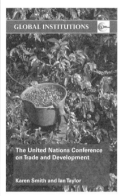

A much-needed new examination of the United Nations Conference on Trade and Development (UNCTAD), fully covering its history and current activities. Ian Taylor and Karen Smith present a clear overview to an organization that is at times overlooked and seen to belong to a bygone era. All the key areas are covered by accessibly written chapters.

Contents
Introduction 1. Historical background 2. UNCTAD's secretariat structure 3. Research, analysis and major publications 4. "Golden years," 1960s–1970s 5. Crisis, retreat and reinvention, 1980s–onwards 6. The multilateral trading system and the future: where does UNCTAD fit into the WTO? 7. Conclusion

May 2007: 216x138mm: 152pp
Hb: 978–0–415–37020–2: **£65.00**
Pb: 978–0–415–37019–6: **£14.99**

NEW TITLE
A Crisis in Global Institutions?
Multilateralism and international security

Edward Newman, United Nations University, Tokyo

This volume considers if there is a crisis in global institutions which address security challenges, exploring the sources of these challenges and how multilateralism might be more viably constituted to cope with contemporary and future demands.

Contents
1. Introduction 2. Defining the crisis of multilateralism in the area of international peace and security 3. Sources of the crisis of multilateralism 4. Emerging alternatives to the existing values and institutions of multilateralism 5. New multilateralism? Towards a "post-Westphalian" model of multilateralism 6. Conclusion

June 2007: 234x156: 184pp
Hb: 978–0–415–41164–6: **£65.00**
Pb: 978–0–415–41165–3: **£16.99**

Routledge
Taylor & Francis Group

To order any of these titles
Call: +44 (0) 1264 34 3071
Fax: +44 (0) 1264 34 3005
Email: book.orders@routledge.co.uk

For further information visit:
www.routledge.com/politics

GLOBAL INSTITUTIONS SERIES

NEW TITLE
The International Monetary Fund
Politics of conditional lending

James Raymond Vreeland, Yale University, USA

Where did the IMF come from? What does it do? Why do so many governments participate in its programs and what are their effects? How can we best reform this key global institution? These are some of the key questions this new text addresses.

Contents
Introduction 1. What is the IMF? 2. Who controls the IMF? 3. Why do governments participate in IMF programs? 4. What are the effects of IMF programs? 5. Do governments comply with IMF arrangements? 6. Reform the IMF? 7. Conclusion

December 2006: 216x138:192pp
Hb: 978–0–415–37462–0: **£65.00**
Pb: 978–0–415–37463–7: **£14.99**

NEW TITLE
The World Trade Organization
Law, economics, and politics

Bernard M. Hoekman, The World Bank, Washington, USA and
Petros C. Mavriodis, Columbia University Law School, USA

Despite – or because of – its success, the WTO has recently become the focus of vociferous protests by anti-globalization activists. This book separates the facts from the propaganda and provides an accessible overview of the WTO's history, structure and policies as well as a discussion of the future of the organization. It also confronts the criticisms of the WTO and assesses their validity.

Contents
Introduction 1. A brief history of the world trading system 2. The WTO in a nutshell 3. The GATT 4. Services and intellectual property 5. Dispute settlement, transparency and plurilateral agreements 6. Developing countries and the WTO 7. Whither the trading system after Doha: deadlock as an opportunity?

June 2007: 216x138mm: 160pp
Hb: 978–0–415–41458–6: **£70.00**
Pb: 978–0–415–41459–3: **£19.99**

Routledge
Taylor & Francis Group

To order any of these titles
Call: +44 (0) 1264 34 3071
Fax: +44 (0) 1264 34 3005
Email: book.orders@routledge.co.uk

For further information visit:
www.routledge.com/politics

GLOBAL INSTITUTIONS SERIES

NEW TITLE
The World Economic Forum
A multi-stakeholder approach to global governance

Dr Geoffrey Allen Pigman, Bennington College, Vermont, USA

This book explores the paradoxes and unique characteristics of the World Economic Forum, highlighting contemporary issues and debates on global governance, economic development, and corporate social responsibility.

Contents
1. A Multi-stakeholder approach: an historical overview 2. Purposes public and private: how the Forum works 3. The Forum in contemporary global society: theoretical questions 4. generating knowledge today: WEF meetings in 2005 5. Discourse, research and action: technology and the initiatives 6. Engaging the critics 7. The Forum looking ahead

December 2006: 216x138: 208pp
Hb: 978–0–415–70203–4: **£65.00**
Pb: 978–0–415–70204–1: **£14.99**

NEW TITLE
The International Committee of the Red Cross
A neutral humanitarian actor

David P. Forsythe, University of Nebraska-Lincoln, USA and
Barbara Ann J. Rieffer-Flanagan, Central Washington University, USA

The International Committee of the Red Cross analyses international humanitarian action as practiced by the International Red Cross. This entails explaining its history and structure as well as examining contemporary field experience and broad diplomatic initiatives related to its principal tasks.

Contents
1. The historical development of the ICRC 2. ICRC organization and management 3. The ICRC and international humanitarian law
4. Humanitarian assistance and restoration of family ties 5. Detention visits 6. The future of the ICRC

April 2007: 216x138: 144pp
Hb: 978–0–415–34613–9: **£65.00**
Pb: 978–0–415–34151–6: **£14.99**

Routledge
Taylor & Francis Group

To order any of these titles
Call: +44 (0) 1264 34 3071
Fax: +44 (0) 1264 34 3005
Email: book.orders@routledge.co.uk

For further information visit:
www.routledge.com/politics